Divorce

in Georgia

*Simple Answers to
Your Legal Questions*

Douglas G. Andrews, Esq.
Richard A. Sanders Jr., Esq.

Addicus Books
Omaha, Nebraska

An Addicus Nonfiction Book

ISBN 978-193880381-9

Typography Jack Kusler

This book is not intended to serve as a substitute for an attorney. Nor is it the author's intent to give legal advice contrary to that of an attorney.

Library of Congress Cataloging-in-Publication Data

Andrews, Douglas G., 1947– author.
 Divorce in Georgia : simple answers to your legal questions / Douglas G. Andrews, J.D.; Richard A. Sanders Jr., J.D.
 pages cm
 Includes bibliographical references and index.
 ISBN 978-1-938803-81-9 (alk. paper)
 1. Divorce—Law and legislation—Georgia. I. Sanders, Richard A., Jr., 1982- author. II. Title.

KFG100.A96 2015
346.75801'66—dc23

2015008998

Addicus Books, Inc.
P.O. Box 45327
Omaha, Nebraska 68145
www.AddicusBooks.com
Printed in the United States of America
10 9 8 7 6 5 4 3 2 1

Much, if not most, of what we do is mindful of the love and support we receive from our families. We are each blessed with a wife who tolerates our deficiencies and late hours; they hold down the fort in our absence, living our marriage vows, working through the issues that arise in every relationship and in any family, but remembering there is a solution to every problem if you put your spouse first, your family second, and yourself last. Therefore, this book is dedicated to Pam Andrews and Crystal Sanders.

Contents

Acknowledgments

Marriage is life's greatest partnership. And for my life, I have been blessed with the greatest partner, Pam. There is no doubt in my mind that if Pam had not been at my side for the past forty-six years, my life, and that of our family, would not have been as happy, as productive, or as successful. Pam has always had the confidence that we could achieve our goals, that we could solve our challenges, and that we could keep love for family as our best legacy to them.

Pam's confidence is our partnership's greatest asset and her love is my greatest resource. Though few may be willing to admit it, the woman who shares our life is the most important factor to enable each of us to be a better man than we could ever be without her. Thank you, Pam, for being you. Thank you for being mine.

Doug Andrews, Esq.

I thank my parents, Richard and Vickie Sanders, for all the love, support, and encouragement along the way and for making it possible for me to pursue my dream of becoming a lawyer. I thank my wife, Crystal Sanders, for keeping me grounded and being there to lift me up whenever times get tough and for giving me my two precious angels, Ryleigh and Mackenzie: They are my world.

I also extend my thanks to the greatest mentor that I could ask for, Doug Andrews. Mr. Andrews has taught me to be the lawyer that I am today, but, even more than that, he has helped mold me into the person that I am. I am not sure where my career or life would be without all these wonderful people. So thank you!

Richard A. Sanders Jr., Esq.

Introduction

We receive many calls from people who have general questions about divorce. Most calls start off with some variation of "I think I need a divorce and I don't know where to start." Clearly, folks in a stressful, life-changing situation need to be put on the right track sooner rather than later.

Therefore, the need for this information in this book was obvious. Equally obvious was that we could never talk to every one of those bewildered, floundering, and hurting souls, so this book is our effort. We wanted to create a place where folks could get their questions answered, in confidence and, with confidence, take the next step, be it reconciliation, separation, or divorce.

This book is not intended to provide definitive answers to every divorce question possible. Nor is it intended to be a self-help, how-to book. This book is intended to be a resource for those individuals who are either going through a divorce or are contemplating a divorce. It's a starting point. Years of family law practice have taught us this important fact, among others: Divorce is almost never simple, easy, or painless. More often, it is complicated, and sometimes messy...not because anyone in their right mind wants it that way, but emotions are involved and conflicting. And, sadly, some folks are not then in their right minds, either.

It is wise to have a lawyer help you and guide you through the process. Someone very knowledgeable once told me, "There is a lawyer for every budget." So, before proceeding without a lawyer because you cannot hire the best, contact every attorney in your city until you find one to fit your budget and with whom you feel comfortable.

1

Understanding the Divorce Process

Divorce isn't such a tragedy. A tragedy's staying in an unhappy marriage, teaching your children the wrong things about love.

Nobody ever died of divorce.

–Jennifer Weiner, *Fly Away Home*

At a time when your life can feel like it's in utter chaos, sometimes the smallest bit of predictability can bring a sense of comfort. The outcome of many aspects of your divorce may be unknown and this can cause the greatest fear and anxiety. But there is one part of your divorce that does have some measure of predictability, and that is the divorce process itself.

Your life will be stressful enough, maybe even overflowing with the drama of the breakup. Avoid throwing gasoline on the burning relationship. Do not think for a moment that it is okay to hook up with someone else, just because you are separated. Sex by a person still married, with a person not his or her spouse, is adultery and is not justified by mere separation. You owe it to yourself to end the marriage by a final decree of divorce before you begin another intimate relationship.

More often than not, building a new relationship on the burning embers and ashes of the old one is simply a weak foundation on which to build a new relationship. Having a new love interest radically alters the dynamics of the relationship with the spouse and the efforts at settling the case by agreement. It also often engenders far more effort (and more attorney fees) by your attorney to minimize the consequences of the extramarital relationship on the divorce process.

Most divorces proceed in a step-by-step manner. Despite the uniqueness of your divorce, you can generally count on one phase of your divorce following the next. Sometimes just realizing you are completing stages and moving forward with your divorce can reassure you that it won't go on forever.

Going through a divorce can bring about a new level of anxiety. When your attorney starts talking about "depositions" or "going to trial," you may feel your heart start pounding in fear. But developing a basic understanding of the divorce process will lower your anxiety. Understanding the divorce process can reduce your frustration and help you understand why each step is needed. It will provide you with the basic support that you need so that you can begin preparing for what comes next.

Most importantly, understanding the divorce process will make your experience of the entire divorce easier. Who wouldn't prefer that?

The Divorce Process

Divorce need not be contentious,
but it too often simply is, but not simply so.

The divorce process in Georgia typically involves the following steps.

If you are initiating the divorce:

- Obtain a referral for an attorney who handles family law cases.
- Schedule an appointment with an attorney.
- Prepare questions and gather necessary documents for an initial consultation.
- Meet for an initial consultation with an attorney.
- Pay the attorney a retainer and sign a retainer agreement or pay the initial fee and sign a fee contract.
- Provide requested information and documents to your attorney.
- Take other actions as advised by your attorney, such as opening or closing financial accounts.

- Attorney prepares the summons and petition for dissolution (or complaint for divorce) for your review and signature.
- Attorney files the summons and petition (or complaint) with the clerk of the court.
- Attorney serves the summons and petition (or complaint) on your spouse (who will be referred to as the *respondent* or the *defendant*).
- If immediate relief (such as temporary child support, deciding who stays put or moves out of the family home, spousal support, or attorney fees) is appropriate, your attorney will prepare any necessary motions (or requests for the court to act) for your review and signature and files these with the court. Your attorney will obtain a court date and will have these documents served on your spouse (the respondent or defendant).

If you have been served with divorce papers:

- Obtain a referral for an attorney who handles family law cases.
- Schedule an appointment with an attorney.
- Prepare questions and gather necessary documents for an initial consultation.
- Meet for an initial consultation with an attorney.
- Pay the attorney a retainer and sign a retainer agreement or pay the initial fee and sign a fee contract.
- Provide requested information and documents to your attorney.
- Take other actions as advised by your attorney, such as opening or closing financial accounts.
- Attorney prepares a response to the summons and petition (or *complaint*) for your review and signature. (Sometimes this will include a counterclaim for a divorce.)
- Attorney files your response with the clerk of the court within thirty days of service of the petition (or complaint) and summons on you.

- If you are served with requests for immediate relief, your attorney prepares your response to these motions.

After an action has been commenced and the response filed:

- With the assistance of your attorney, you need to prepare financial disclosure documents (income and expense declaration and preliminary schedule of assets and debts). Georgia refers to this document as a *financial affidavit.*

- Negotiations may begin regarding temporary custody and visitation, child and spousal support, payment of obligations, and attorney fees.

- Attorney prepares motions for any requests for relief during the divorce process not previously made.

- If there are minor children, the parties comply with any local rules or court orders to attend divorcing parent orientation and to participate in mandatory mediation.

- The court holds hearing(s) on requests for temporary relief (so the parties can know who has to do what during the divorce).

- Either the parties reach an agreement or the court rules on temporary orders.

- Temporary order is prepared by one attorney, approved as to form by other attorney, and submitted to the judge for signature.

- Both sides conduct discovery—the process designed to obtain information regarding all relevant facts—and commence the process to exchange valuations of all assets, including expert opinions if needed.

- You confer with your attorney to review facts, identify issues, assess strengths and weaknesses of case, review strategy, and develop a settlement proposal.

- Spouses, with the support of their attorneys, attempt to reach agreement through written proposals, mediation, settlement conferences, or other forms of negotiation.

If you reach an agreement on all issues, then:

- One attorney prepares marital settlement agreement and necessary judgment paperwork.
- Both parties and their attorneys sign agreement and all necessary paperwork.
- Judgment paperwork is filed with the court.
- Either the parties waive the court date or the court holds a brief, final hearing.
- Judgment is entered and you will be divorced.
- Your attorney completes necessary orders and helps facilitate any transfers of property, assets, or debts.

If you are *unable* to reach an agreement on all issues, then:

- Your attorney completes all necessary discovery to bring the case to its trial-ready point.
- Your attorney files a request to obtain trial dates.
- If agreement has been reached on any issues, your attorney prepares a stipulation on those issues. All other issues are set for trial.
- You work with your attorney to prepare your case for trial.
- Your attorney prepares witnesses, trial exhibits, legal research on contested issues, pretrial motions, trial briefs, direct and cross-examination of witnesses, opening statements, witness subpoenas, and your closing argument.
- You meet with your attorney for final trial preparation.
- Trial is held. In Georgia, either spouse may demand jury trial, if desired.
- The judge or jury issues a judgment or decision and directs this ruling to be prepared as an order of the court.
- The judge signs the final order dissolving your marriage.
- The attorneys help facilitate any transfers until all agreed terms are satisfied.

(Your posttrial rights are discussed in the chapter on appeals.)

1.1   Must I have an attorney to get a divorce in Georgia?

You are not required to have an attorney to obtain a divorce in Georgia. A person who proceeds in a legal matter without a lawyer is referred to as being *pro se* (pronounced pro-say), which translates to "on one's own."

You should be very cautious about proceeding in a divorce case without a lawyer. You would not perform a medical operation on yourself just because you found a book that described the procedure and someone gave you a scalpel. Legal work is no different. The best advice is to hire a lawyer who is trained in these matters.

If you are considering proceeding without an attorney, at a minimum you should have an initial consultation with an attorney to discuss your rights and duties under the law. You may have certain rights or obligations about which you are unaware. Meeting with a lawyer can help you decide whether to proceed on your own.

If your case involves children, alimony, significant property, or debts, you should avoid proceeding on your own. The more issues in your case, the more complicated your case will be. It's always better to have matters handled correctly the first time. A judge, frustrated by a party without a lawyer, may not be the judge you would want ruling in your case.

1.2   What is my first step?

Find a law firm that handles divorces as a regular part of its law practice. The best recommendations come from people who have knowledge of a lawyer's experience and reputation.

Even if you are not ready to file for divorce, call to schedule an appointment right away to obtain information about protecting yourself and your children. Even if you are not planning to file for divorce, your spouse might be.

Ask what documents you should bring to your initial consultation. Make a list of questions to bring to your first meeting. Start making plans for how you will pay your attorney to begin work on your case. Legal fees may be expensive, but if you think hiring an experienced lawyer is expensive, then try hiring an inexperienced one!

1.3 Is Georgia a *no-fault* state or do I need grounds for a divorce?

Georgia, like most states, is a *no-fault* divorce state. This means that neither you nor your spouse is required to prove that the other is "at fault" in order to be granted a divorce. Factors such as infidelity, cruelty, or abandonment are not necessary to receive a divorce in Georgia. Rather, it is necessary to prove that the marriage is "irretrievably broken" with "no hope of reconciliation" and that you and your spouse are living in a "*bona fide* state of separation" to have the marriage dissolved.

The testimony of either you or your spouse is likely to be sufficient evidence for the court to rule that the marriage should be dissolved. This testimony, usually given by the spouse who filed for the divorce, will state that you two have been separated, that you two are living in a "*bona fide* state of separation," and that the marriage is irretrievably broken and that there is no hope of reconciliation.

However, Georgia still recognizes "fault" grounds and parties can claim and be granted a divorce based on fault grounds. Georgia recognizes twelve fault grounds for divorce:

- Intermarriage by persons within the prohibited degrees of consanguinity (related by blood) and affinity (related by marriage)
- Mental incapacity at the time of the marriage
- Impotency at the time of marriage
- Force, menace, duress, or fraud in obtaining the marriage
- Pregnancy of the wife by a man other than the husband, at the time of the marriage, unknown by the husband
- Adultery by either of the parties after marriage
- Willful and continued desertion by either of the parties for the term of one year
- The conviction of either party for an offense involving moral turpitude and under which he or she is sentenced to imprisonment in a penal institution for a term of two years or longer
- Habitual intoxication

- Cruel treatment, which shall consist of the willful infliction of pain, bodily or mental, upon the complaining party, such as reasonably justifies apprehension of danger to life, limb, or health
- Incurable mental illness
- Habitual drug addiction

1.4 Do I have to get divorced in the same state I got married in?

No. You should seek a divorce in the state in which you reside. Regardless of where you were married, you may seek a divorce in Georgia if the jurisdictional requirements are met.

1.5 What is the minimum time a person must have lived in Georgia to be eligible to file for divorce here?

Either you or your spouse must have been a "*bona fide* resident" of Georgia (or "domiciled" in Georgia) for at least six months to meet the residency requirement for a divorce in Georgia.

Georgia allows an exception to this requirement for U.S. military members. If a person has been stationed at a U.S. military post in Georgia for at least twelve months pursuant to military orders immediately before the filing, then the divorce action may be filed in Georgia.

If neither party meets the "*bona fide* resident/domiciliary" requirement or the twelve-month assignment requirement, other legal options are available. If you do not meet the six-month residency requirement (nor qualify under the service members exception), talk to your attorney about options, such as a petition for separate maintenance or a protection order.

1.6 My spouse has told me "I will never give you a divorce." Can I get one in Georgia without my spouse's consent?

Yes. Georgia does not require that your spouse "agree to" a divorce. If your spouse threatens to "not give you a divorce," know that in Georgia this is likely to be an idle threat without any basis in the law.

Under Georgia law, to obtain a divorce you must be able to prove that your marriage is "irretrievably broken and there is no hope of reconciliation." Evidence of this will be your testimony on the witness stand. In short, it is not necessary to have your spouse agree to the divorce or to allege the specific difficulties that arose during the marriage to obtain a divorce in Georgia. If one spouse shows the marriage is broken, the judge must grant the divorce.

1.7 Can I divorce in Georgia if my spouse lives in another state?

Yes, provided you have met the residency requirements for living in Georgia for six months (or, if military, stationed at a military installation in Georgia for twelve months or more), you can file for divorce here even if your spouse lives in another state.

Discuss with your attorney the facts that will need to be proven and the steps necessary to give your spouse proper notice to ensure that the court will have jurisdiction over your spouse. Your attorney can counsel you on whether it is possible to proceed with the divorce.

1.8 How can I get a divorce when I don't know where my spouse now lives?

Georgia law allows you to proceed with a divorce even if you do not know the current address of your spouse. First, take serious, diligent action to attempt to locate your spouse. Contact family members, friends, former co-workers, or anyone else who might know your spouse's whereabouts. Utilize resources on the Internet that are designed to help locate people. Document and keep a record of your efforts.

Let your attorney know of the efforts you have made to attempt to find your spouse. Inform your attorney of your spouse's last known address, as well as any work address or other address where this person may be found. Once your attorney attempts to give notice to your spouse without success, it is possible to ask the court to proceed with the divorce by giving notice through publication in a newspaper.

Although your divorce may be granted following service of notice by publication in a newspaper, you may not be able to get other court orders, such as those for child support or alimony, without giving personal notice to your spouse. Talk to your attorney about your options and rights if you don't know where your spouse is living.

1.9 I just moved to a different county. Do I have to file in the county where my spouse lives?

Yes. Georgia requires you to file a divorce in the county where your spouse resides. However, a party may file a divorce in his or her own county of residence if the other party has moved from that same county within six months before the date of the filing of the divorce and this county was the site of the marital domicile at the time of the separation of the parties.

1.10 I immigrated to Georgia. Will my immigration status stop me from getting a divorce?

If you meet the residency requirements for divorce in Georgia, you can get a divorce in Georgia despite your immigration status. Talk to your immigration lawyer about the likelihood of a divorce leading to immigration challenges or its effect on your immigration status. The *Immigrations and Customs Enforcement (ICE)* is always on the lookout for someone who has a "sham" marriage that was used to qualify for immigration or a visa. Prepare to prove your marriage was entered into in good faith.

If you are a victim of domestic violence, tell your lawyer. You may be eligible for a change in your immigration status under the *Violence Against Women Act*. An immigration attorney can provide details and information as to whether you are covered by the law, and there may be other provisions of law to help you.

1.11 I want to get divorced in my Indian tribal court. What do I need to know?

Each tribal court has its own laws governing divorce. Requirements for residency, grounds for divorce, and the laws regarding property, alimony, and children can vary substantially from state law. Some tribes have very different laws governing the grounds for your divorce, removal of children from the home, and cohabitation.

Contact an attorney who is knowledgeable about the law in your tribal court for legal advice on pursuing a divorce in your tribal court or on the requirements for recording a divorce obtained in state court with the clerk of the tribal court.

1.12 Is there a waiting period for a divorce in Georgia?

Yes. Georgia has a waiting period, but this period varies based on the circumstances of your divorce. If both parties provide written consent, then a divorce may be granted as soon as thirty-one days after the defendant is determined to have been given legal notice of the divorce.

Otherwise, if there is no waiver or answer by the other spouse, a divorce may be granted forty-six days after the defendant is determined to have been given legal notice of the divorce, unless the time for the defendant's response has been extended by court order.

If the defendant cannot be found and he or she is provided legal notice by publication, the divorce may be granted sixty-one days after the date of the first publication.

1.13 What is a *divorce complaint?*

A *divorce complaint,* also referred to as a *complaint for dissolution of marriage* (or a *petition for divorce*), is a document signed by the person filing for divorce and filed with the clerk of the court to initiate the divorce process. The complaint, sometimes referred to as a *petition,* will state in general terms what the plaintiff is asking the court to order. *See* the appendix for an example.

1.14 What is a *verification page?*

A *verification page,* also referred to as an *affidavit,* is a document that is signed under oath that states that the claims in the complaint are true and accurate. Georgia requires a complaint for divorce to be accompanied by a verification. *See* the appendix for an example.

1.15 My spouse said the divorce was filed last week, but my lawyer says there's nothing on file at the courthouse. What does it mean to "file for divorce"?

When lawyers use the term *filing* they are ordinarily referring to filing a legal document at the courthouse, such as delivering a complaint for divorce to the clerk of the court. Sometimes a spouse who has hired a lawyer to begin a divorce action asserts, "I've filed for divorce," meaning, usually, that the spouse has begun the process by engaging an attorney, who *will* file the divorce action, but it might not yet have been taken to the courthouse.

1.16   If we both want a divorce, does it matter who files?

Maybe, maybe not. In the eyes of the court, the *plaintiff* (the party who files the complaint initiating the legal process of the divorce) and the *defendant* (the other spouse) are not seen differently by virtue of which party filed.

Your attorney may advise you to file first or to wait until your spouse files, depending upon the overall strategy for your case and your circumstances. For example, if there is a concern that your spouse will begin transferring assets upon learning about your plans for divorce, your attorney might advise you to seek a temporary restraining order to protect against such an action, without giving prior notice to your spouse. However, if you are separated from your spouse but have a beneficial temporary arrangement, your attorney may counsel you to wait for your spouse to file.

Sometimes, a question of *venue* (what county is proper for filing of the divorce) may be more important than who files first. Generally, whoever files first (if separated more than six months), usually must file in the county of the other spouse. So, if you want to be served with a petition for divorce in your county of residence, you might let the other spouse file first. But the other spouse might know the rules of venue, too, and might delay in filing—hoping you will give in first.

Ask your attorney to explain the consequences of such matters and help you decide whether venue is more important than getting the divorce filed sooner rather than later.

1.17   Can I stop the newspaper from printing a story or publishing a legal notice of the filing or granting of my divorce?

Documents filed with the court, such as a divorce complaint, are a matter of public record. Newspapers have a right to access this information, but unless you or your spouse are public figures or celebrities, your divorce will not likely be newsworthy enough to have a reporter write a story on you.

However, if you do not know the whereabouts of your spouse, then you will have to publish legal notice of the divorce in the classified ads section of the newspaper. Newspapers that publish such notices typically do so within a week of the date that documents are filed with the clerk of the court.

In rare cases, a divorce file may be kept private, referred to as being *sealed* or *under seal* if the court orders it.

1.18 Is there a way to avoid embarrassing my spouse and not have the sheriff serve the divorce papers at the workplace?

Talk to your attorney about the option of having your spouse sign a document known as an *acknowledgment of service*. The signing and filing of this document with the court can eliminate the need to have your spouse personally served by the sheriff. Additionally, it is sometimes possible to hire a private process server, who can serve the divorce papers on your spouse at an appropriate time, away from the work site. If the spouse has an attorney, that attorney might accept service on behalf of your spouse.

1.19 Should I sign an *acknowledgment of service* even if I don't agree with what my spouse has written in the complaint for divorce?

Signing the acknowledgment of service does not mean that you agree with anything your spouse has stated in the divorce complaint or anything that your spouse is asking for in the divorce. Signing the acknowledgment of service substitutes only for having the sheriff personally hand you the documents. You do not waive the right to object to anything your spouse has stated in the complaint for divorce.

Follow your attorney's advice on whether and when to sign an acknowledgment of service.

1.20 Why should I contact an attorney right away if I have received divorce papers?

If your spouse has filed for divorce, it is important that you obtain legal advice as soon as possible. Even if you and your spouse are getting along, having independent legal counsel can help you make decisions now that could affect your divorce and your life later.

After your spouse has filed for divorce, a temporary hearing can be scheduled at any time. It is possible you will receive only a few days' notice of a temporary hearing. You will be better prepared for a temporary hearing if you have already hired an attorney.

After your voluntary appearance or acknowledgment of service has been filed with the court or you have been served by the sheriff, a written answer responding to your spouse's divorce complaint must be filed with the court within thirty days.

1.21   What is an *ex parte* court order?

An *ex parte* court order is obtained by one party going to the judge to ask for something without giving prior notice or an opportunity to be heard by the other side. *Ex parte* is Latin for "on one side only."

With the exception of restraining orders, judges are generally reluctant to sign *ex parte* orders. Ordinarily, the court will require the other side to have notice of any requests for court orders, and a hearing before the judge will be held.

An *affidavit,* which is a written statement sworn under oath, is usually required before a judge will sign an *ex parte* order. In some cases, the judge will require the party requesting the *ex parte* order to appear in person and testify under oath. *Ex parte* orders are generally limited to emergency situations such as requests for temporary restraining orders and protection orders.

When an *ex parte* order is granted, the party who did not request the order will have an opportunity to have a subsequent hearing before the judge to determine whether the order should remain in effect. If the judge does grant an *ex parte* order, then there are certain rules that say when this subsequent hearing must be held; you should discuss these special rules with your attorney.

1.22   What is a *motion*?

A *motion* is a request that the judge enter a court order of some type. For example, your attorney may file a written motion with the court asking for temporary custody and child support.

Some motions are made to handle certain procedural aspects of your case, such as a motion for a continuance asking that a court date be changed or a motion for extension of time asking that the court extend a deadline. In some cases a motion may be made orally rather than in writing. An oral motion is usually made when an issue arises during the course of a court hearing or trial.

1.23 Once my complaint for divorce is filed, how long will it take before a temporary hearing is held to decide what happens with our child and our finances while the divorce is pending?

The answer depends on the judge who is assigned to your case and that judge's schedule. There are also certain rules for emergency or *ex parte* hearings that should be discussed with your attorney. However, in most cases, a temporary hearing will be held within thirty days of your divorce being filed with the court, presuming your spouse can be located to be given notice.

1.24 How much notice will I get if my spouse seeks a temporary order?

Georgia law requires that you receive notice of the temporary hearing at least fifteen days before the date of the hearing. However, you should be aware that this can always be modified by the judge.

1.25 During my divorce, what am I responsible for doing?

Your attorney will explain what actions you should take to assist in your divorce and the actions that will help you reach the best possible outcome.

You will be asked to do the following:

- Keep in regular contact with your attorney
- Update your attorney regarding any changes in your contact information, such as address, phone numbers, and e-mail address
- Provide your attorney with all requested documents
- Provide requested information in a timely manner
- Complete forms and questionnaires

- Appear in court on time
- Be direct about asking any questions you might have
- Tell your attorney your thoughts on settlement or what you would like the judge to order in your case.
- Remain respectful toward your spouse throughout the process
- Comply with any temporary court orders, such as restraining or support orders
- Advise your attorney of any significant developments in your case
- Not post anything on social media (such as Facebook) that you would not want to be used as Exhibit A used against you in court. Keep your private business private.

By doing your part in the divorce process, you enable your attorney to partner with you for a better outcome while also lowering your attorney fees.

1.26   I'm worried that I won't remember to ask my lawyer about all of the issues in my case. How can I be sure I don't miss anything?

Write down all of the topics you want to discuss with your attorney, including what your goals are for the outcome of the divorce. The sooner you clarify your goals, the easier it will be for your attorney to support you to get what you want. Realize that your attorney will think of some issues that may not have occurred to you. Your lawyer's experience will be helpful in making sure nothing important is forgotten. Use the Divorce Issues Checklist, on the following pages, as a helpful reference.

Divorce Issues Checklist

Issue	Notes
Dissolution of marriage—divorce	
Custody of minor children	
Removal of children from jurisdiction	
Parenting plan (time, transportation, etc.)	
Child support	

Divorce Issues Checklist (Continued)

Issue	Notes
Extraordinary expenses warranting a deviation in child support	
Summer child support	
Life insurance to fund unpaid child support	
Automatic withholding for support	
Child-care expenses	
Health insurance on minor children	
Uninsured medical expenses for minor children	
Private school tuition for children	
College expenses for children	
Health insurance on the parties	
Real property: rentals, cabins, commercial property, etc. (deed, refinancing, sale)	
Marital expenses associated with real estate	
Time-shares	
Retirement plans (401k, Simple IRA, TSA, etc.), possible QDROs	
Federal or military pensions	
Businesses	
Bank accounts	
Investments	
Stock options	
Premarital or nonmarital assets	
Premarital or nonmarital debts	
Pets	

Divorce Issues Checklist (Continued)

Issue	Notes
Personal property division: including motor vehicles, recreational vehicles, campers, airplanes, collections, furniture, electronics, tools, household goods, etc.	
Exchange date for personal property	
Division of marital debt	
Property settlement	
Alimony	
Life insurance to fund unpaid alimony	
Sums owed under temporary order	
Tax exemptions for minor children	
IRS Form 8332 for claiming children as dependents	
Filing status for tax returns for last/current year	
Restoration of former name	
Attorney fees	

It is important to maintain contact with your attorney. If you forget something and think of it later, then send your attorney an e-mail or call the office.

1.27 My spouse has all of our financial information. How will I be able to prepare for negotiations and trial if I don't know the facts or have the documents?

Once your divorce has been filed with the court, your attorney may proceed with a process known as "discovery." Through discovery, your attorney can demand that your spouse provide these documents and information so that you can prepare your case.

Also, it is in your best interest to request the records directly from the source—go get copies of your bank statements and bills.

1.28 My spouse and I both want our divorce to be amicable. How can we keep it that way?

You and your spouse are to be commended for your willingness to cooperate while focusing on moving through the divorce process. This will not only make your lives easier and save you money on attorney fees, but it is also more likely to result in an outcome you are both satisfied with. It is usually better for the two parties to decide their personal business than let twelve strangers or a busy judge make rapid decisions about your business on information constrained by the rules of evidence.

Find an attorney who understands your goal to reach a settlement and encourage your spouse to do the same. Cooperate with the prompt exchange of necessary information. Then ask your attorney about the options of mediation and negotiation for reaching an agreement. Even if you are not able to settle all of the issues in your divorce, these actions can increase the likelihood of agreement on many of the terms of your divorce decree.

1.29 Can I get a different judge?

Talk to your attorney about the reasons you want a different judge. If you believe that your judge has a conflict of interest, such as being a close friend with your spouse, you may have a basis for asking the judge to be "recused" in order to allow another judge to hear the case. The fact that you just don't like your judge (or you think the judge does not like you) is not a legally sufficient reason to remove that judge. If this is the case, you are more than likely stuck and you might need to reevaluate your strategy.

1.30 How long will it take to get my divorce?

The more you and your spouse are in agreement, the faster your divorce will conclude. At a minimum, there will be a thirty-one-day wait from the date of either service of the divorce complaint on the spouse who did not file for divorce or from the date the non-filing spouse filed a an acknowledgment of service with the court.

Assuming all issues, such as custody, support, property, and debts, are completely settled between you and your spouse, a final hearing can be held after the thirty-one-day waiting period.

1.31   What is the significance of my divorce being final?

The finality of your divorce decree, sometimes referred to as the *final judgment* and *decree of divorce,* is important for many reasons. It can affect your right to remarry, your eligibility for health insurance from your former spouse, and your filing status for income taxes.

1.32   When does my divorce become final?

Your divorce becomes final on the date that the divorce decree (*final judgment* and *decree of divorce*) is entered by the court. In most cases, this will be the day the judge signs your divorce decree and it is filed of record by the clerk of the court.

However, please remember that under Georgia law a party has thirty days to appeal an order of the court. Please review the chapter on appeals for further discussion.

1.33   Can I start using my former name right away and how do I get my name legally restored?

You may begin using your former name at any time, provided you are not doing so for any unlawful purpose, such as to avoid your creditors. Many agencies and institutions, however, will not alter their records without a court order changing your name. Due to Homeland Security issues, your name must be the same on state driver license records and the Social Security Administration.

If you want your former name restored, let your attorney know so that this provision can be included in your divorce decree or final judgment and decree of divorce. If you want to change your legal name after the divorce and have not provided for it in your decree, it will be necessary for you to undergo a separate legal action for a name change.

The process for changing your name back will be the same as when you changed it when you got married.

2

Coping with Stress during the Divorce Process

This, too, shall pass...
like a kidney stone, perhaps, but it will pass.

It may have been a few years ago. Or it may have been many years ago. Perhaps it was only months. But, when you said "I do," you meant it. Like most people getting married, you planned to be a happily married couple for life.

But things happen. Life brings change. People change. Or your love-struck eyes finally open to the reality of a person you did not know all that well. Whatever the circumstance, you now find yourself considering divorce. The emotions of divorce run from one extreme to another as you journey through the process. You may feel relief and ready to move on with your life. On the other hand, you may feel emotions that are quite painful. Anger. Fear. Sorrow. A deep sense of loss or failure.

Remember, it is important to find support for coping with all these strong emotions. Because going through a divorce can be an emotional time, having a clear understanding of the divorce process and what to expect will help you make better decisions. And, when it comes to decision making, search inside yourself to clarify your intentions and goals for the future. Let these intentions be your guide.

The stress of a marital breakup is the beginning of the end of the pain in a troubled marriage. The pain you will be feeling is the stress of your marriage transitioning to the stress of the divorce. This, too, shall pass.

2.1   My spouse left home weeks ago. I don't want a divorce because I feel our marriage can be saved, but the stress is getting to me. What should I do?

Uncertainty can cause stress. A licensed professional counselor may be advisable to help you learn to cope with the stress. As you work yourself through this life-changing event, stress will not disappear, but will morph over time through each phase of the divorce process. Stress cannot be eliminated, but you can learn to keep it under control, so it does not control you.

Consulting an attorney often leads to stress reduction because a plan can be formulated and you will know your legal rights and options.

Whether you want a divorce or not, there may be important actions for you to take now to protect your assets, credit, home, children, and future right to support.

Even if you decide not to file for a divorce at this time, your spouse might surprise you with a complaint for divorce. If your spouse files for divorce, a temporary hearing could be heard in just a matter of days. It is best to be prepared with the support of an attorney. Furthermore, you should understand that in Georgia it takes only one party to testify that the marriage is irretrievably broken with no hope of reconciliation for the judge to grant the divorce.

2.2   The thought of going to a lawyer's office to talk about divorce is more than I can bear. I canceled the first appointment I made because I just couldn't do it. What should I do?

Many people going through a divorce are dealing with lawyers for the first time and feel anxious about the experience. Ask a trusted friend or family member to go with you. He or she can support you by writing down your questions in advance, taking notes for you during the meeting, and helping you to remember what the lawyer said after the meeting is concluded. It is very likely that you will feel greatly relieved just to be better informed.

If going to the office is too overwhelming then try to set up a phone conference or e-mail some of your questions to your lawyer. By discussing initial issues this way, it may make it easier for you to have a face-to-face meeting.

This is also why it's important to find an attorney that you can trust and one that makes you feel comfortable.

2.3 There is some information about my marriage that I think my attorney needs, but I'm too embarrassed to discuss it. Must I tell the attorney?

Your attorney has an ethical duty to maintain confidentiality. Past events in your marriage are matters that your lawyer is obligated to keep private.

Attorneys who practice divorce law are accustomed to hearing a lot of intimate information about families. Although it is deeply personal to you, it is unlikely that anything you tell your attorney will be a shock.

Although it may feel uncomfortable for a short moment, it is important that your attorney have complete information so that your interests can be fully protected. If speaking directly about these facts still seems too hard, consider putting them in a letter or an e-mail—sometimes just writing things down will help.

The best advice is to tell your attorney everything. Nothing is worse for an attorney than being blindsided by the other side because the client was not upfront and honest about everything. Additionally, your attorney may have a different strategy depending on the particular facts and circumstances.

2.4 I'm unsure about how to tell our children about the divorce, and I'm worried I'll say the wrong thing. What's the best way?

How you talk to your children about the divorce will depend upon their ages and development. Changes in your children's everyday lives, such as a change of residence or one parent leaving the home, are far more important to them. Information about legal proceedings and meetings with lawyers are best kept among adults. In fact, Georgia has adopted certain guidelines regarding what can be discussed with your children. Remember, it is best to avoid involving your children as much as possible.

Simpler answers are best for young children. Avoid giving them more information than they need. Use the adults in your life as a source of support to meet your own emotional needs.

After the initial discussion, keep the door open to further talks by creating opportunities for them to talk about the divorce. Use these times to acknowledge their feelings and offer support. Always assure them that the divorce is not their fault and that they are still loved by both you and your spouse, regardless of the divorce.

2.5   My youngest child seems very depressed about the divorce, the middle one is angry, and my teenager is skipping school. How can I cope?

A child's reaction to divorce can vary depending upon his or her age and other factors. Some may cry and beg for a reconciliation, and others may act out. Reducing conflict with your spouse, being a consistent and nurturing parent, and making sure both of you remain involved with your children are all actions that can support your children regardless of how they are reacting to the divorce.

Support groups for children whose parents are divorcing are available at many schools and religious communities. A school counselor can also provide support. If more help is needed, confer with a therapist experienced in working with children.

2.6   I am so frustrated by my spouse's "Disneyland parent" behavior. Is there anything I can do to stop this?

Feelings of guilt, competition, or remorse sometimes lead a parent to be tempted to spend parenting time in trips to the toy store and special activities. Other times they can result in an absence of discipline in an effort to become the favored parent or to make the time "special."

Shift your focus from the other parent's behavior to your own, and do your best to be an outstanding parent during this time. This includes keeping a routine for your child for family meals, bedtimes, chores, and homework. Encourage family activities, as well as individual time with each child when it's possible.

During a time when a child's life is changing, providing a consistent and stable routine in your home can ease anxiety and provide comfort.

2.7 Between requests for information from my spouse's lawyer and my own lawyer, I am totally overwhelmed. How do I manage gathering all of this detailed information by the deadlines imposed?

First, simply get started. Often the thought about a task is worse than the job itself.

Second, break it down into smaller tasks. Perhaps one evening you gather your tax returns and on the weekend you work on your monthly living expenses.

Third, let in support. Ask that friend of yours who just loves numbers to come over for an evening with her calculator to help you get organized.

Finally, communicate with your attorney. Your attorney or paralegal may be able to make your job easier by giving you suggestions or help. It may be that essential information can be provided now and the details submitted later.

2.8 I am so depressed about my divorce that I'm having difficulty getting out of bed in the morning to care for my children. What should I do?

See your health-care provider. Feelings of depression are common during a divorce. You also want to make sure that you identify any physical health concerns, too.

Although feelings of sadness are common during a divorce, more serious depression means it's time to allow some professional support.

Your health and your ability to care for your children are both essential. Follow through on recommendations by your health-care professionals for therapy, medication, or other measures to improve your wellness.

2.9 I know I need help to cope with the stress of the divorce, but I can't afford counseling. What can I do?

You are wise to recognize that divorce is a time for letting in support. You can explore a number of options, including:

- Meeting with a member of the clergy or lay chaplain

- Joining a divorce support group
- Turning to friends and family members
- If budget is a concern, contact a social agency that offers counseling services on a sliding-fee scale.

If none of these options are available, look again at your budget. You may see that counseling is important enough that you decide to find a way to increase your income or lower your expenses to support this investment in your well-being.

2.10 I'm the one who filed for divorce, but I still have loving feelings toward my spouse and feel sad about divorcing. Does this mean I should dismiss my divorce?

Strong feelings of caring about your spouse often persist after a divorce is filed. Whether to proceed with a divorce is a deeply personal decision. Although feelings can inform us of our thoughts, sometimes they can also cause us to not look at everything there is to see in our situation. Oftentimes when we are apart from something familiar, we tend to focus only on the good times and somehow manage to forget all the bad times—it's called selective memory. It is understandable that you are having these feelings, but before making a decision, try to remember everything—the good and the bad.

Have you and your spouse participated in marriage counseling? Has your spouse refused to seek treatment for an addiction? Are you worried about the safety of you or your children if you remain in the marriage? Can you envision yourself as financially secure if you remain in this marriage? Is your spouse involved in another relationship?

The answer to these questions can help you clarify whether to consider reconciliation. Talk to your therapist, coach, or spiritual advisor to help determine the right path for you.

2.11 Will my lawyer charge me for the time I spend talking about my feelings about my spouse and my divorce?

It depends. If you are paying your attorney by the hour, expect to be charged for the time your attorney spends talking with you. If your attorney is being paid a flat rate for handling your divorce, the time spent talking with you may be included in the fee. However, it is important to remember that your attorney has a job to do and this job is not to be your therapist.

Sometimes your attorney has to tell you things that may not be easy to hear, but may be in your best interest. Lastly, it may be cheaper to hire a therapist rather than pay expensive legal fees for your attorney to listen to you talk about your feelings.

2.12 My lawyer doesn't seem to realize how difficult my divorce is for me. How can I get him to understand?

Everyone wants support and compassion from the professionals who are helping them during a divorce. Speak frankly with your attorney about your concerns. It may be that your attorney does not see your concerns as being relevant to his or her job of getting your desired outcome in the divorce. Your willingness to improve the communication will help your attorney understand how best to support you in the process and will help you understand which matters are best left for discussion with your therapist or a supportive friend.

You hire an attorney to look out for your best interest. Your attorney should advise and inform you. Most people hire an attorney because they want someone to look at their case objectively and guide them in the right direction. Divorces are difficult on everyone and sometimes it takes the guidance from someone who is not as emotionally invested to help resolve the conflict. Your attorney should be invested in your case and you should feel that he or she is looking out for your best interest, but sometimes that means being very blunt.

2.13 I've been told not to speak ill of my spouse in front of my child, but I know she's doing this all the time. Why can't I just speak the truth?

Two wrongs don't make a right. It can be devastating for your child to hear you bad-mouthing his or her other parent. What your child needs is permission to love both of you, regardless of any bad parental behavior. The best way to support your child during this time is to encourage a positive relationship with the other parent. If your spouse is speaking ill of you in front of your child then let your attorney know. You should never stoop to the other parent's level. The best advice is to rise above the pettiness.

Georgia has certain rules of conduct that should be followed regarding parenting time. Georgia has enacted these rules of conduct in hopes of relieving the minor child of embroilment in his or her parents' controversies and disputes.

2.14 Nobody in our family has ever been divorced and I feel really ashamed. Will my children feel the same way?

Making a change in how you see your family identity is huge for you. The best way to help your children is to establish a sense of pride in their new family and to look forward to the future with a real sense of possibility.

Your children will have an opportunity to witness you overcoming obstacles, demonstrating independence, and moving forward in your life despite challenges. You can be a great teacher to them during this time by demonstrating pride in your family and in yourself.

Unfortunately, more and more children are growing up in divorced households. It might be unique to your family dynamic, but your children will have friends whose parents are divorced and your children will adapt, with your help.

2.15 I am terrified of having my deposition taken. My spouse's lawyer is very aggressive, and I'm afraid I'm going to say something that will hurt my case.

A deposition is an opportunity for your spouse's attorney to gather information and to assess the type of witness you will be if the case proceeds to trial. Feeling anxious about your deposition is normal. However, regardless of the personality of the lawyers, most depositions in divorces are quite uneventful.

Remember that your attorney will be seated by your side at all times to support you. Ask to meet with your lawyer in advance to prepare for the deposition. If you are worried about certain questions that might be asked, talk to your attorney about them. Think of it as an opportunity, and enlist your attorney's support in being well prepared.

2.16 I am still so angry at my spouse. How can I be expected to sit in the same room during a settlement conference?

If you are still really angry at your spouse, it may be beneficial to postpone the conference for a later time. You might also consider seeking some counseling to support you with coping with your feelings of anger.

Another option might be "shuttle" negotiations or "caucus negotiations." With this method, you and your attorney remain in one room while your spouse and his or her attorney are in another. Settlement offers are then relayed between the attorneys throughout the negotiation process. By shifting your focus from your angry feelings to your goal of a settlement, it may be easier to proceed through the process.

2.17   I'm afraid I can't make it through court without having an emotional breakdown. How do I prepare?

A divorce trial can be a highly emotional time, calling for lots of support. Some of these ideas may help you through the process:

- Meet with your attorney or the firm's support staff in advance of your court date to prepare you for court.
- Ask your attorney whether there are any documents you should review in preparation for court, such as your deposition.
- Visit the courtroom in advance to get comfortable with the surroundings.
- Ask your attorney about having a support person with you on your court date.
- Ask yourself what the worst thing is that could happen and consider what options you would have if it did.
- Avoid alcohol, eat healthfully, exercise, and have plenty of rest during the period of time leading up to the court date. Each of these will help you to prepare for the emotions of the day.
- Plan what you intend to wear in advance. Small preparations will lower your stress.
- Visualize the experience going well. Picture yourself sitting in the witness chair, giving clear, confident, and truthful answers to easy questions.
- Arrive early at the courthouse and make sure you have a plan for parking your car if you are not familiar with the area.

- Take slow, deep breaths. Breathing deeply will steady your voice, calm your nerves, and improve your focus.

Your attorney will be prepared to support you throughout the proceedings. By taking these steps, you can increase the ease of your experience.

2.18   I am really confused. One day I think I've made a mis-take, the next day I know I can't go back, and a few minutes later I can hardly wait to be single again. Some days I just don't believe I'm getting divorced. What's happening?

What you are experiencing is normal for a person going through divorce. Denial, transition, and acceptance are common passages for a person going through a divorce. One moment you might feel excited about your future and a few hours later you think your life is ruined.

What can be helpful to remember is that you may not pass from one stage to the next in a direct line. Feelings of anger or sadness may build up in you long after you thought you had moved on. Similarly, your mood might feel bright one day as you think about your future plans, even though you still miss your spouse.

Going through a divorce is a lot like dealing with the death of a loved one. We recover from death of a relationship much like we recover from the actual death of a loved one. Healing comes in stages. After all, a divorce is the death of your marriage.

Taking good care of yourself is essential during this period of your life. What you are going through requires a tremendous amount of energy. Allow yourself to experience your emotions, but also continue moving forward with your life. These steps will help your life get easier day by day.

3

Working with an Attorney

Litigation is a team effort, but it need not be a blood sport.
The goal of the team is success.
Success is not measured in pain inflicted on the other team.

If there is only one thing you can be sure of in your divorce, it's that you will be given plenty of advice. Well-intentioned neighbors, cousins, and complete strangers will be happy to tell you war stories about their ex or about their sister who got divorced in another state. Many will insist they know what you should do, even though they haven't the vaguest notion of the facts of your case or the law in Georgia.

But there is one person whose advice will matter to you: your attorney. Your attorney should be your trusted and supportive advocate at all times throughout your divorce. The advice of your attorney can affect your life for years to come. You will never regret taking the time and energy to choose the right attorney to provide you with the wisest advice.

Consider your relationship with your attorney as a partnership for pursuing what is most important to you. With clear and open attorney-client communication, you'll have the best outcome possible and your entire divorce will be less stressful.

By working closely with the right lawyer, you can trust the professional advice you receive and simply thank your cousin Millie for sharing.

3.1 Where do I begin looking for an attorney for my divorce?

There are many ways to find a divorce attorney. Ask people you trust, friends, and family members who have gone through a divorce if they thought they had a great attorney (or if their former spouse did!). If you know professionals who work with attorneys, ask for a referral to an attorney who is experienced in family law.

Go online. Many attorneys have websites that provide information on their practice areas, professional associations, experience, and philosophy.

Consult your local bar association to find out whether they have a referral service. Be sure to specify that you are looking for an attorney who handles divorces.

3.2 How do I choose the right attorney?

Choosing the right attorney for your divorce is an important decision. Your attorney should be a trusted professional with whom you feel comfortable sharing information openly. He or she should be a person you can trust and a zealous advocate for your interests.

You will rely upon your attorney to help you make many decisions throughout the course of your divorce. You will also entrust your legal counsel to make a range of strategic and procedural decisions on your behalf.

Consultation for a divorce might be your first meeting with an attorney. Know that attorneys want to be supportive and to fully inform you. Feel free to seek all of the information you need to help you feel secure in knowing you have made the right choice.

Find an attorney who practices primarily in the family law area. Although many attorneys handle divorces, it is likely you will have more effective representation from an attorney who already knows the fundamentals of divorce law in Georgia.

Determine the level of experience you want in your attorney. Consider the qualities in an attorney that are important to you. Even the most experienced and skilled attorney is not right for every client. Ask yourself what it is that you are really looking for in an attorney so you can make your choice with these standards in mind.

It is important that you be confident in the attorney you hire. If you're unsure about whether the attorney is really listening to you or understanding your concerns, keep looking until you find one who will. Your divorce is an important matter. It's critical that you have a professional you can trust.

However, don't think that trust means the attorney will tell you everything you want to hear. You need an attorney who will give an honest assessment of your case and will let you know if you have unrealistic expectations.

3.3   Should I interview more than one attorney?

The answer depends on what you are looking for. Sometimes the first choice is the right choice and sometimes it isn't. Be willing to interview more than one attorney, but, if you're comfortable with the first and feel that he or she is the attorney you want, then hire him or her. Every lawyer has different strengths, and it is important that you find the one that is right for you. Sometimes it is only by meeting with more than one attorney who you see clearly who will best be able to help you reach your goals in the way you want.

Changing attorneys in the middle of litigation can be stressful and costly. It is wise to invest energy at the outset in making the right choice.

3.4   My spouse says because we're still friends we should use the same attorney for the divorce. Is this a good idea?

Even the most amicable of divorcing couples usually have differing interests. For this reason, it is never recommended that an attorney represent both parties to a divorce. In most cases, an attorney is ethically prohibited from representing two people with conflicting interests who are in dispute.

Sometimes, couples have reached agreements without understanding all of their rights under the law. A client often will benefit from receiving further legal advice on matters such as tax considerations, retirement, and health insurance issues.

It is not uncommon for one party to retain an attorney and for the other party not to do so. In such cases, the party with the attorney files the complaint, and agreements reached between the parties are typically sent to the spouse for approval prior to any court hearing. If your spouse has filed for divorce and said that you do not need an attorney, you should nevertheless meet with a lawyer for advice on how proceeding without a lawyer could affect your legal rights.

3.5   What information should I take with me to the first meeting with my attorney?

Attorneys differ on the amount of information they like to see at an initial consultation. If a court proceeding, either a divorce or a protection order, has already been initiated by either you or your spouse, it is important to take copies of any court documents.

If you have a prenuptial or postnuptial agreement with your spouse, that is another important document for you to take at the outset of your case.

If you intend to ask for support, either for yourself or for children, documents evidencing income of both you and your spouse will also be useful. These might include:

- Recent pay stubs
- Individual and business tax returns, W-2s, and 1099s
- Bank statements showing deposits
- A statement of your monthly budget

Your attorney will ask you to complete a questionnaire at the time of your first meeting. Ask whether it is possible to do this in advance of your meeting. This can allow you to provide more complete information and to make the most of your appointment time with the lawyer.

If your situation is urgent or you do not have access to these documents, don't let it stop you from scheduling your appointment with an attorney. Prompt legal advice about your rights is often more important than having detailed financial information in the beginning. Your attorney can explain to you the options for obtaining these financial records if they are not readily available to you.

3.6 What unfamiliar words might an attorney use at the first meeting?

Law has a language all its own, and attorneys sometimes lapse into "legalese," forgetting that nonlawyers may not recognize words used daily in the practice law. Some words and phrases you might hear include:

- *Dissolution of marriage*—the divorce
- *Plaintiff*—person who files the divorce complaint
- *Defendant*—person who did not file the divorce complaint
- *Jurisdiction*—authority of a court to make rulings affecting a party
- *Service*—process of notifying a party about a legal filing
- *Discovery*—process during which each side provides information to the other
- *Decree*—the final order entered in a divorce

Never hesitate to ask your attorney the meaning of a term. Your complete understanding of your lawyer's advice is essential and necessary for you to partner with your lawyer as effectively as possible.

There are many more terms and phrases that are commonly used by attorneys in divorces than what's listed above. It might be a good idea to read through the glossary of terms at the back of this book before your meeting with your attorney. This section may also be useful to review during the course of your divorce.

3.7 What can I expect at an initial consultation with an attorney?

Most attorneys will ask that you complete a questionnaire prior to the meeting. With few exceptions, attorneys are required to keep confidential all information you provide.

The nature of the advice you get from an attorney in an initial consultation will depend upon whether you are still deciding whether you want a divorce, whether you are planning for a possible divorce in the future, or whether you are ready to file for divorce right away.

During the meeting, you will have an opportunity to provide the following information to the attorney:

- A brief history of the marriage
- Background information regarding yourself, your spouse, and your children
- Your immediate situation
- Your intentions and goals regarding your relationship with your spouse
- What information you are seeking from the attorney during the consultation

You can expect the attorney to provide the following information to you:

- The procedure for divorce in Georgia
- A preliminary list of the issues important in your case
- A preliminary assessment of your rights and responsibilities under the law
- Background information regarding the firm
- Information about fees and billings

Although some questions may be impossible for the attorney to answer at the initial consultation because additional information or research is needed, the initial consultation is an opportunity for you to ask all of the questions you have at the time of the meeting. It is important to remember that many of your questions or concerns regarding the divorce cannot be answered at an initial consultation. In order for most of your concerns to be addressed, your attorney will have to have a deeper understanding of the facts of your case and your desires. It is also important to remember that a lot of your concerns can be addressed in many different ways. This is why it is important for you to find an attorney you are comfortable with.

Lastly, the things that you want addressed at a consultation may not be able to be addressed without your hiring the attorney so he or she can stand behind the answers provided or the course of conduct recommended.

3.8 Can I take a friend or family member to my initial consultation?

Yes. Having someone present during your initial consultation can be a source of great support. You might ask him or her to take notes on your behalf so that you can focus on listening and asking questions. Remember that this is your consultation, however, and it is important that the attorney hear the facts of your case directly from you.

3.9 What exactly will my attorney do to help me get a divorce?

Your attorney will play a critical role in helping you get your divorce. You will be actively involved in some of the work, while other actions will be taken behind the scenes at the law office, the law library, or the courthouse.

Your attorney may perform any of the following tasks on your behalf:

- Assess the case to determine which court has jurisdiction to hear the matter
- Develop a strategy for advising you about all aspects of your divorce, including the treatment of assets and matters regarding children
- Prepare legal documents for filing with the court
- Conduct discovery to obtain information from the other party, which could include depositions, requests for production of documents, and written interrogatories
- Appear with you at all court appearances, depositions, and conferences
- Schedule all deadlines and court appearances
- Support you in responding to information requests from your spouse
- Inform you of actions you are required to take
- Perform financial analyses of your case
- Conduct legal research
- Prepare you for court appearances and depositions
- Prepare your case for hearings and trial, including preparing exhibits and interviewing witnesses

- Advise you regarding your rights under the law
- Counsel you regarding the risks and benefits of negotiated settlement as compared to proceeding to trial

As your advocate, your attorney is entrusted to take all of the steps necessary to represent your best interest in the divorce.

3.10 What professionals might the court appoint to work with my attorney?

In some cases where custody or parenting time issues are seriously disputed, the court may appoint a guardian *ad litem,* that is, one whose duty it is to represent the best interest of the child. A guardian *ad litem* has the responsibility to investigate you and your spouse as well as the needs of your child. She or he may then be called as a witness at trial to testify regarding any relevant observations.

Another expert who could be appointed by the court is a psychologist. The role of the psychologist will depend upon the purpose for which she or he was appointed. For example, the psychologist may be appointed to perform a child-custody evaluation, which involves assessing both parents and the child, or this expert may be ordered to evaluate one parent to access the a child's safety while spending time with that parent.

3.11 I've been divorced before and I don't think I need an attorney this time; however, my spouse is hiring one. Is it wise to go it alone?

Having gone through a prior divorce, it's likely that you have learned a great deal about the divorce process as well as your legal rights. However, there are many reasons why you should be extremely cautious about proceeding without legal representation.

It is important to remember that every divorce is different. The length of the marriage, whether there are children, the relative financial situation of you and your spouse, as well as your age and health can all affect the financial outcome in your divorce.

The law may have changed since your last divorce. Some aspects of divorce law are likely to change each year. New laws get passed and new decisions get handed down by the

Georgia Supreme Court and the Georgia Court of Appeals that affect the rights and responsibilities of people who divorce.

When asking yourself this question, it might be helpful to hear a quote from Abraham Lincoln that goes something like this: "A man who represents himself has a fool for a client."

3.12   Can I take my children to meetings with my attorney?

It's best to make other arrangements for your children when you meet with your attorney. Your attorney will be giving you a great deal of important information during your conferences and it will benefit you to give your full attention.

It's also recommended that you take every measure to keep information about the legal aspects of your divorce away from your children. Knowledge that you are seeing an attorney can add to your child's anxiety about the process. It can also make your child a target for questioning by the other parent about your contacts with your attorney.

Most law offices are not designed to accommodate young children and are ordinarily not "child-proofed." For both your child's well-being and your own peace of mind, explore options for someone to care for your child when you have meetings with your attorney.

3.13   What is the role of the *paralegal* or *legal assistant* in my attorney's office?

A *paralegal* or *legal assistant* is a trained legal professional whose duties include providing support for you and your attorney. Working with a paralegal can make your divorce easier because he or she is likely to be very available to help you. It can also lower your legal costs, because the hourly rate for paralegal services is less than the rate for attorneys.

A paralegal is prohibited from giving legal advice. It is important that you respect the limits of the role of the paralegal if he or she is unable to answer your question because it calls for giving a legal opinion. However, a paralegal can answer many questions and provide a great deal of information to you throughout your divorce.

Paralegals can help you by receiving information from you, reviewing documents with you, providing you with updates on your case, and answering questions about the divorce process that do not call for legal advice.

If you have questions or concerns regarding your case and your attorney is not available, then you should ask the paralegal. The paralegal is there to assist you and your attorney. Many times the paralegal can answer questions about your case that don't require legal answers and therefore will allow your attorney more time to focus on the legal issues in your case.

3.14 My attorney is not returning my phone calls. What can I do?

You have a right to expect your phone calls to be returned by your lawyer. Here are some options to consider:

- Ask to speak to your attorney's paralegal or assistant.
- Send an e-mail or fax telling your attorney that you have been trying to reach him or her by phone and explaining the reason it is important that you receive a call.
- Ask the receptionist to schedule a phone conference for you to speak with your attorney at a specific date and time.
- Schedule a meeting with your attorney to discuss both the issue needing attention as well as your concerns about the communication.

Your attorney wants to provide good service to you. If your calls are not being returned, take action to get the communication with your attorney back on track.

The number-one complaint that clients have regarding attorneys is their failure to return calls. However, it is important to understand that most attorneys are very busy and that you are probably not their only client.

Understand that your divorce involves many steps and that most attorneys will call only if something has happened in your case. If you just want a status update, then ask your attorney's paralegal or assistant. If you have an emergency, then relay that to your attorney's staff and send an e-mail to follow up.

It is important to remember that every minute your attorney spends returning your call and being concerned if you are happy is a minute that he or she is not working on trying to resolve your case.

3.15 How do I know when it's time to change lawyers?

This should be a last resort because changing lawyers is costly. You will incur legal fees for your new attorney to review information that is already familiar to your current attorney. You will spend time giving much of the same information to your new attorney as you gave the one you have discharged. A change in lawyers often results in delays in the divorce.

The following are questions to ask yourself when you're deciding whether to stay with your attorney or seek new counsel:

- Have I spoken directly to my attorney about my concerns?
- When I expressed concerns, did my attorney take action accordingly?
- Is my attorney open and receptive to what I have to say?
- Am I blaming my attorney for bad behavior of my spouse or opposing counsel?
- Have I provided my attorney the information needed for taking the next action?
- Does my attorney have control over the complaints I have, or are they ruled by the law or the judge?
- Is my attorney keeping promises for completing action on my case?
- Do I trust my attorney?
- What would be the advantages of changing attorneys when compared to the costs?
- Do I believe my attorney will support me to achieve the outcome I'm seeking in my divorce?

Every effort should be made to resolve challenges with your attorney. Contact your attorney directly and let him or her know your concerns and that you are considering changing attorneys. Give your attorney a chance to respond and to explain the situation to you. If you have made this effort and the situation remains unchanged, it may be time to switch attorneys.

4

Attorney Fees and Costs

Three marketplace principles to remember:
You get what you pay for.
'Tis better to buy for quality than for price alone.
You rarely regret buying the best quality you can afford.

Any time you make a major investment, you want to know what the cost is going to be and what you are getting for your money. Investing in quality legal representation for your divorce is no different.

The cost of your divorce might be one of your greatest concerns. Because of this, you will want to be an intelligent consumer of legal services. You want quality, but you also want to get the best value for the fees you are paying.

Legal fees for a divorce can be costly and the total expense not always predictable. But there are many actions you can take to control and estimate the cost. Develop a plan early on for how you will finance your divorce. Speak openly with your attorney about fees from the outset. Learn as much as you can about how you will be charged. Most divorce attorneys will provide you with a written fee agreement, but if one is not provided then insist on one.

By being informed, aware, and wise, your financial investment in your divorce will be money well spent to protect your future.

4.1 Can I get free legal advice from a lawyer over the phone?

Every law firm has its own policy regarding attorneys talking to people who are not yet clients of the firm. Most questions about your divorce are too complex for an attorney to give a meaningful answer during a brief phone call. The free consultations that are offered are usually for you to explain your situation to the attorney and have the attorney decide if he or she can handle your case or not and to explain the fees to handle the matter.

Questions about your divorce require a complete look at the facts, circumstances, and background of your marriage. To obtain good legal advice, it's best to schedule a meeting with an attorney who handles divorces and one who will stand behind the advice that he or she provides.

4.2 Will I be charged for the initial consultation with a lawyer?

It depends. Some attorneys give free consultations, whereas others charge a fee. Whether fees are charged or not will usually depend on the length and depth of the consultation. An initial assessment of whether the attorney can help or not should be free, but an in-depth analysis of your case and issues should entail a fee. If you take your car to a mechanic and ask the mechanic to do an in-depth inspection of your vehicle and tell you what is needed to fix the car, then the mechanic will charge you. A visit with a lawyer follows this same premise. When scheduling your appointment, you should be told the amount of the fee. Payment is ordinarily due at the time of the meeting.

4.3 Will I be expected to give money to the attorney after our first meeting? If so, how much?

If your attorney charges for the meeting, be prepared to make payment at the time of your meeting. At the close of your meeting, the attorney may tell you the amount of the retainer or fee needed by the law firm to handle your divorce. The retainer or fee is paid after you have decided to hire the attorney, the attorney has accepted your case, and you are ready to proceed.

4.4   What exactly is a *retainer* and how much will mine be?

A *retainer* is a sum paid to your attorney in advance for services to be performed and costs to be incurred in your divorce. It's an advance credit for services that will be charged by the hour.

If your case is accepted by the law firm, expect the attorney to request a retainer following the initial consultation. The amount of the retainer may vary from hundreds of dollars to several thousand dollars, depending upon the nature of your case. Contested custody, divorces involving businesses, or interstate disputes, for example, are all likely to require higher retainers.

Other factors that can affect the amount of the retainer include the nature and number of the disputed issues, the degree of conflict between the parties, and the anticipated overall cost of the litigation.

4.5   What is a *flat fee* and how much will mine be?

A *flat fee* is just what it sounds like. Many family law attorneys handle cases on a flat-fee basis. Your attorney will explain these fees and what is covered under each set of fees. Some attorneys find this fee structure more client friendly, because the client will know what work will be performed and what the cost will be in advance.

The amount of the flat fee may vary from hundreds of dollars to several thousand dollars, depending upon the nature of your case. Contested custody, divorces involving businesses, or interstate disputes, for example, are all likely to require higher flat fees.

Other factors that can affect the amount of the flat fee include the nature and number of the disputed issues, the degree of conflict between the parties, and the anticipated overall cost of the litigation.

4.6   What are typical hourly rates for a divorce lawyer?

In Georgia, attorneys who practice in the divorce area charge from $125 per hour to more than four times that rate. The rate your attorney charges may depend upon factors such as skills, reputation, experience, and what other attorneys in the area are charging.

If you have a concern about an attorney's hourly rate, but you would like to hire the firm with which the attorney is associated, consider asking to work with an associate attorney in the firm who is likely to charge a lower rate. Associates are attorneys who ordinarily have less experience than the senior partners. However, they are often trained by the senior partners, with varying levels of experience, and should be fully capable of handling your case.

4.7   How much does it cost to get a divorce?

The cost of your divorce will depend upon many factors. Some attorneys perform divorces for a flat fee, but most charge by the hour. A flat fee is a fixed amount for the legal services being provided. A flat fee is more likely to be used when there are no children of the marriage and the parties have agreed upon the division of their property and debts. More and more attorneys are charging set fees in a tiered approach—you will pay an initial fee, and then you will pay a set flat fee for each phase of your divorce, if necessary.

It is important that your discussion of the cost of your divorce begin at your first meeting with your attorney. It is customary for family law attorneys to request a retainer, also known as a *fee advance,* or to request full payment of the flat fee, prior to beginning work on your case.

Be sure to ask your attorney what portion, if any, of the retainer is refundable if you do not continue with the case or terminate your relationship with the attorney. These issues, and others regarding fees, should be addressed in your fee agreement.

4.8   What factors will impact how much my divorce will cost?

Although it is difficult to predict how much your legal fees will be, the following are some of the factors that affect the cost:

- Whether there are children
- Whether child custody is agreed upon
- Whether there are novel legal questions
- Whether a pension plan or retirement account will be divided between the parties

- The nature of the issues contested
- The number of issues agreed to by the parties
- The cooperation of the opposing party and opposing counsel
- Whether there are litigation costs, such as fees for expert witnesses or court reporters
- The hourly rate (or flat fees) of the attorney

Communicating with your attorney regularly about your legal fees will help you to have a better understanding of the overall cost as your case proceeds.

4.9   Can I make payments to my attorney?

Every law firm has its own policies regarding payment arrangements for divorce clients. Often these arrangements are tailored to the specific client. Most attorneys will require a substantial retainer, or a substantial amount of the flat fee, to be paid at the outset of your case. Some attorneys may accept monthly payments in lieu of the retainer. Others may require monthly payments or request additional retainers as your case progresses. Ask frank questions of your attorney to have clarity about your responsibility for payment of legal fees. Make sure to read your fee agreement because these types of questions should be answered in it.

4.10   I don't have much money, but I need to get a divorce as quickly as possible. What should I do?

If you have some money and want to divorce as soon as possible, consider some of these options:

- Borrow the legal fees.
- Charge the legal fees on a low-interest credit card.
- Talk with your attorney about using money held in a joint account with your spouse.
- Find an attorney who will work with you on a monthly payment basis.

- Ask your attorney about your spouse paying for your legal fees.

- Contact Georgia Lawyer Referral/Legal Services. Let them know you have some ability to pay and ask for help finding a lawyer who will take your case for a reduced fee.

Even if you do not have the financial resources to proceed with your divorce at this time, consult with an attorney to learn your rights and to develop an action plan for steps you can take between now and the time you are able to proceed.

Often, there are measures you can take right away to protect yourself until you have the money to proceed with your divorce.

4.11   I don't have any money and I need a divorce. What are my options?

If your income is very low and your assets are few, you may be eligible to obtain a divorce at no cost or minimal cost through one of the following organizations:

- Georgia Legal Services (commonly referred to as "Legal Aid")

- Georgia State Bar Association Lawyer Referral/Legal Services

These organizations have a screening process for potential clients, as well as limits on the nature of the cases they take. The demand for their services is also usually greater than the number of attorneys available to handle cases. Consequently, if you are eligible for legal services from one of these programs, you should anticipate being on a waiting list. If you believe you might be eligible for participation in one of these programs, inquire early to increase your opportunity to get the legal help you are seeking.

There is an attorney for every budget. If you need an attorney, then there is one who is willing to work for you. Contact every attorney in town and tell them your situation. Someone should be able to help—either by reducing their fees or rates or by allowing you to make payments.

4.12   Is there anything I can do on my own to get support for my children if I don't have money for a lawyer for a divorce?

Yes. If you need support for your children, contact Child Support Services of Georgia for help in obtaining a child-support order. Although they cannot help you with matters such as custody or property division, they can pursue support from your spouse for your children. Call toll-free (844) 694-2347, or visit their website at http://dcss.dhs.georgia.gov.

4.13   I've been turned down by programs providing free legal services. How can I get the money to pay for a lawyer?

There are a number of options to consider when it looks as though you are without funds to pay an attorney. First, look again. Ask yourself whether you have closely examined all sources of funds readily available to you. Sometimes you may have overlooked money that you might be able to access.

Next, talk to your family members and friends. Often those close to you are concerned about your future and would be very pleased to support you in your goal of having your rights protected. Although this may be uncomfortable to do, remember that most people will appreciate that you trusted them enough to ask for their help. If the retainer (or initial fee) is too much money to request from a single individual, consider whether a handful of people might each be able to contribute a lesser amount to help you reach your goal of hiring a lawyer.

If your case is not urgent, consider developing a plan for saving the money you need to proceed with a divorce. Your attorney may be willing to receive and hold monthly payments until you have paid an amount sufficient to pay the initial retainer.

Consider taking out a loan or charging your retainer (or initial fee) on a credit card.

Under certain circumstances, an attorney might be willing to be paid from the proceeds of a property settlement. If you and your spouse have acquired substantial assets during the marriage, you may be able to find an attorney who will wait to be paid until the assets are divided at the conclusion of the divorce.

Lastly, talk to the attorney you want to hire. Let him or her know your financial situation and try to set up a payment plan. Most attorneys want to help and will be willing to work with you. But remember, you get what you pay for.

4.14 I agreed to pay my attorney a substantial retainer to begin my case. Will I still have to make monthly payments?

Ask your attorney what will be expected of you regarding payments on your account while the divorce is in progress. Make sure you understand if monthly payments on your account will be expected, whether it is likely that you will be asked to pay additional retainers, and whether the firm charges interest on past-due accounts. Regular payments to your attorney can help you avoid having a tremendously burdensome legal bill at the end of your case.

4.15 My lawyer gave me an estimate of the cost of my divorce and it sounds reasonable. Do I still need a written fee agreement?

Absolutely. Insist upon a written agreement with your attorney. This is essential not only to define the scope of the services for which you have hired your lawyer, but also to ensure that you have clarity about matters such as your attorney's hourly rate (or additional flat fees), whether you will be billed for certain costs such as copying, and when you can expect to receive statements on your account.

A clear fee agreement reduces the risk of misunderstandings between you and your attorney. A fee agreement should provide you both with a clear understanding about your promises to each other so that your focus can be on the legal services being provided rather than on disputes about your fees.

If your attorney is spending time trying to collect money from you, then that is time that he or she is not focusing on your divorce and what really matters. With a written fee agreement in place, your attorney will have more time to devote to your case.

4.16 How will I know how the fees and charges are accumulating?

Be sure your written fee agreement with your attorney is completely clear about how you will be informed regarding the status of your account. If your attorney agrees to handle your divorce for a flat fee, your fee agreement should clearly set forth what is included in the fee. If your attorney charges a flat fee, then there is a chance that you will not receive a bill regarding the work performed for the flat fee. However, this should all be addressed in your fee agreement.

Most attorneys charge by the hour for handling divorces. At the outset of your case, be sure your written fee agreement includes a provision for the attorney to provide you with regular statements of your account. It is reasonable to ask that these be provided monthly.

Review the statement of your account promptly after you receive it. Check to make sure there are no errors, such as duplicate billing entries. If your statement reflects work that you were unaware was performed, call for clarification. Your attorney's office should welcome any questions you have about services it provided.

Your statement might also include filing fees, court reporter fees for transcripts of court testimony or depositions, copy expenses, or interest charged on your account.

If several weeks have passed and you have not received a statement on your account, call your attorney's office to request one. Legal fees can mount quickly, and it is important that you stay aware of the status of your legal expenses.

4.17 What other expenses are related to the divorce litigation besides lawyer fees?

Talk to your attorney about costs other than the attorney fees. Ask whether it is likely there will be filing fees, court reporter expenses, fees for subpoenas, or expert-witness fees. Expert-witness fees can be a substantial expenses ranging from hundreds to thousands of dollars, depending upon the type of expert and the extent to which he or she is involved in your case. Many attorneys will bill or charge clients for postage, copying, travel time, and other costs that the attorney might have.

Speak frankly with your attorney about these costs so that together you can make the best decisions about how to use your budget for the litigation. Make sure that all the costs are addressed in your fee agreement and that you understand exactly what you will pay for.

4.18 Who pays for the experts such as the guardian *ad litem*, the appraiser, the accountant, and the psychologist?

Costs for the services of experts, whether appointed by the court or hired by the parties, are ordinarily paid for by the parties.

In the case of the guardian *ad litem,* who may be appointed to represent the best interest of your children, the amount of the fee will depend upon how much time this professional spends. A guardian *ad litem* may charge an hourly fee. The judge often orders this fee to be shared by the parties. However, depending upon the circumstances, one party can be ordered to pay the entire fee. If you can demonstrate *indigence,* that is, a very low income and no ability to pay, the county may be ordered to pay your share of the guardian *ad litem* fee. If a guardian *ad litem* is appropriate in your case, then discuss the specifics with your attorney. Some courts have guardian programs that help pay some of the guardian *ad litem* expenses.

Psychologists either charge by the hour or can set a flat fee for a certain type of evaluation. Again, the court can order one party to pay this fee or both parties to share the expense. It is not uncommon for a psychologist to request payment in advance and hold the release of an expert report until fees are paid.

The fees for many experts, including appraisers and accountants, will vary depending upon whether the individuals are called upon to provide only a specific service such as an appraisal, or whether they will need to prepare for giving testimony and appear as a witness at trial.

You should discuss the need for an expert with your attorney. Ask if your case requires this additional expense or if there are other ways to have the evidence presented without incurring these additional costs.

4.19   Will my attorney charge for phone calls and e-mails?

Unless your case is being handled on a flat-fee basis, you should expect to be billed for phone calls with your attorney. Many of the professional services provided by lawyers are done by phone and by e-mail. This time can be spent giving legal advice, negotiating, or gathering information to protect your interests. These calls and e-mails are all legal services for which you should anticipate being charged by your attorney.

To make the most of your time during attorney phone calls, plan your call in advance. Organize the information you want to relay, your questions, and any concerns to be addressed. This will help you to be clear and focused during the phone call so that your fees are well spent.

Always make sure to review your retainer or fee agreement because these issues should be addressed in this document. The main thing the retainer or fee agreement should address is how much you will be billed for the work your attorney does.

4.20   Will I be charged for talking to the staff at my lawyer's office?

It depends. Check the terms of your fee agreement with your lawyer. Whether you are charged fees for talking to non-lawyer members of the law office may depend upon their role in the office. For example, many law firms charge for the services of paralegals and law clerks.

Remember that nonlawyers cannot give legal advice; therefore, it's important for you to respect their roles. Don't expect the receptionist to give you an opinion regarding whether you will win custody or receive alimony.

Your lawyer's support staff will be able to relay your messages and receive information from you. They may also be able to answer many of your procedural questions. Allowing support from non-attorneys in the firm is one way to control your legal fees, too.

4.21 What is a *litigation budget,* and how do I know if I need one?

If your case is complex and you are anticipating substantial legal fees, ask your attorney to prepare a *litigation budget* for your review. This can help you to understand the nature of the services anticipated, the time that may be spent, and the overall cost. It can also be helpful for budgeting and planning for additional retainers. Knowing the anticipated costs of litigation can help you to make meaningful decisions about which issues to litigate and which to consider resolving through settlement negotiations.

Budgeting for litigation is another reason that many divorce attorneys are moving towards tiered flat-fee billing. This method will allow you to know from the beginning of your case what each phase of the litigation will cost and you can budget accordingly. *See* the Sample Attorney Litigation Fee Hourly Billing Structure in the Appendix, which is for illustrative purposes only. Lawyer fees range from modest to very high.

4.22 What is a *trial retainer* and will I have to pay one?

A *trial retainer* is similar to the initial retainer described previously, but a trial retainer is for the specific purpose of preparing for trial. A trial retainer is a sum of money paid on your account with your attorney when it appears as though your case may not settle and is at risk for proceeding to trial. The purpose of the trial retainer is to fund the work needed to prepare for trial and for services on the day or days of trial.

Confirm with your attorney that any unearned portion of your trial retainer will be refunded if your case settles. Ask your lawyer when a trial retainer might be required in your case so that you can avoid surprise and plan your budget accordingly. Also, review your retainer or fee agreement. This should be addressed in that agreement.

4.23 How do I know whether I should spend the attorney fees my attorney says it will require to take my case to trial?

Deciding whether to take a case to trial or to settle is often the most challenging point in the divorce process. This decision should be made with the support of your attorney.

When the issues in dispute are primarily financial, often the decision about settlement is related to the costs of going to trial. This is the *cost-benefit analysis* that your attorney will refer to. Clarify just how far apart you and your spouse are on the financial matters and compare this to the estimated costs of going to trial. By comparing these amounts, you can decide whether a compromise on certain financial issues and certainty about the outcome would be better than paying legal fees and not knowing how your case will resolve.

This is a decision that you may have to make. Your attorney should go over the good, the bad, and the ugly of your case and hopefully by doing so you will be able to make an informed decision regarding your case.

4.24 If my mother pays my legal fees, will my attorney give her private information about my divorce?

If someone other than you is paying your legal bills, it is important that you clarify with your attorney and with the person paying that you expect your attorney to honor their ethical duty to maintain confidentiality. Without your permission, your attorney should not be disclosing information to others about your case unless you consent to it.

If you do want your attorney to be able to communicate with your family members, advise your attorney of this. Expect to be charged by your attorney for the time spent on these calls or meetings. Regardless of the opinions of the person who pays your attorney fees, your attorney's duty is to remain your zealous advocate.

4.25 Can I ask the court to order my spouse to pay my attorney fees?

Yes. If you want to ask the court to order your spouse to pay any portion of your legal fees, be sure to discuss this with your attorney at the first opportunity. Most attorneys will treat the obligation for your legal fees as yours until the other party has made payment.

If your case is likely to require costly experts and your spouse has a much greater ability to pay these expenses than you, talk to your attorney about the possibility of filing a motion with the court asking your spouse to pay toward these costs while the case is pending.

4.26   What happens if I don't pay my attorney the fees I promised to pay?

The ethical rules for lawyers allow your attorney to withdraw from representation if you do not comply with your fee agreement. Consequently, it is important that you keep the promises you have made regarding your account.

If you are having difficulty paying your attorneys fees, talk with your attorney about payment options. Consider borrowing the funds, using a credit card, or asking for help from friends and family.

Above all, do not avoid communication with your attorney if you are having challenges making payment. Keeping in touch with your attorney is essential for you to have an advocate at all stages of your divorce.

It is important to remember that when you hired your attorney you entered into a contract with him or her for your attorney to provide you with legal services and for you to pay a certain fee for those services. Your attorney-client relationship is no different from any other payment for services in that respect. If your attorney has performed work for you and you have not paid him, then there is a chance that your attorney will sue you for a breach of contract and for payment of services provided.

It is also important to pay your attorney because attorneys talk to one another and if you are a client who has a reputation for not paying, then it might be difficult to find another attorney to represent you.

4.27   Is there any way I can reduce some of the expenses of getting a divorce?

Litigation of any kind can be expensive, and divorces are no exception. The good news is that there are many ways that you can help to control expenses. Here are some of them.

Put it in writing. If you need to relay information that is important but not urgent, consider providing it to your attorney by mail, fax, or e-mail. This creates a prompt and accurate record for your file, and this method allows your attorney to review this information in less time than exchanging phone messages, talking on the phone, and taking notes of the telephone conversation.

Keep your attorney informed. Just as your attorney should keep you up to date on the status of your case, you need to do the same. Keep your attorney advised about any major developments in your life such as plans to move, to have someone move into your home, to change your employment status, or to buy or sell property.

During a divorce, your address, phone number, or e-mail address may change. Be sure to let your attorney know any of these changes as soon as possible. Often, timely advice on the part of your attorney can avoid the need for more costly fees later.

Obtain copies of documents. An important part of litigation includes reviewing documents such as tax returns, account statements, report cards, or medical records. Your attorney will ordinarily be able to request or *subpoena* these items, but such a request may be costly. Many of the documents that your attorney will need may be readily available to you directly upon request. Therefore, if you request the documents, you may be able to save some attorney fees.

Consult your attorney's website. If your attorney has a website, it may be a great source of useful information. The answers to commonly asked questions about the divorce process can often be found there.

Utilize support professionals. Get to know the support staff at your attorney's office. The receptionist, paralegal, legal secretary, or law clerk may have the answer to your question. Only the attorneys in the office are able to give you legal advice, but other professionals in the law office can often provide answers to questions regarding the status of your case. Just as your communication with your attorney, all communication with any professionals in a law firm is required to be kept strictly confidential.

Consider working with an associate attorney. Although the senior attorneys or partners in a law firm may have more experience, you may find that working with the associate attorney is a good option. Hourly rates for an associate attorney are typically lower than those charged by a senior partner. Frequently, the associate attorney has trained under a senior partner and developed excellent skills as well as knowledge of the law. Many associate attorneys are also very experienced.

Discuss with the firm the benefits of working with a senior or an associate attorney in light of the nature of your case, the expertise of the respective attorneys, and the potential cost savings to you.

Leave a detailed message. If your attorney is unavailable and you have a question, then ask one of the other staff members. The staff member may not be able to answer your question, but he or she will be able to relay the question directly to your attorney. If your attorney knows the information you are seeking, he or she can often get the answer before returning your call. This not only gets your answer faster, but also reduces costs.

Discuss more than one matter during a call. It is not unusual for clients to have many questions during litigation. If your question is not urgent, consider waiting to call until you have more than one inquiry. Never hesitate to call to ask any legal questions.

Provide timely responses to information requests. Whenever possible, provide information requested by your attorney in a timely manner. This avoids the cost of follow-up action by your attorney and the additional expense of extending the time in litigation.

Carefully review your monthly statements. Scrutinize your monthly billing statements closely. If you believe an error has been made, contact your attorney's office right away to discuss your concerns.

Remain open to settlement. Be alert to when disagreement with your spouse about smaller sums of money may cost more in legal fees to take to court than the value of what is disputed. By doing your part, you can use your legal fees wisely and control the costs of your divorce.

5

The Discovery Process

Truth is constant and the facts will become known.
He who hides assets or the truth will pay the price to the court.

Interrogatories. Depositions. Subpoena *duces tecum.* Even the words are foreign.

Discovery is one of the least talked about steps in divorce, but it is often among the most important. The discovery process enables you and your spouse to meet on a more level playing field when it comes to settling your case or taking it to trial.

You and your spouse both need the same information if you hope to reach agreement on any of the issues in your divorce. Similarly, the judge must know all of the facts to make a fair decision. The purpose of discovery is to ensure that both you and your spouse have access to the same information. In this way, you can either negotiate a fair agreement or have all of the facts and documents to present to the judge at trial.

The discovery process may seem tedious at times because of the need to obtain and to provide lots of detailed information. Completing it, however, can give tremendous clarity about the issues in your divorce. Trust your attorney's advice about the importance of having the necessary evidence as you complete the discovery process in order to reach your goals in your divorce.

5.1   What is *discovery*?

As mentioned, *discovery* is that part of your divorce process in which the attorneys attempt to learn as much about the facts of your case as possible. Through a variety of methods, both attorneys will request information from you, your spouse, potential witnesses in your case, and third-party data holders. Social media (Facebook, Myspace, Twitter, Instagram, LinkedIn, Pinterest, Meetup, MeetMe, Match.com, eHarmony, Tumblr, Flickr) has become a treasure trove of information on people—don't let it have yours. (*See* question 5.3.)

5.2   What types of discovery might be done by my attorney or my spouse's attorney?

Types of discovery include:

- *Interrogatories*—which are written questions that must be answered under oath
- *Requests for production of documents*—asking that certain documents be provided by you or your spouse
- *Requests for admissions*—asking that certain facts be admitted or denied
- *Subpoena of documents*—which are generally demands for someone to turn over records or documents, including social media providers and cell phone carriers
- *Depositions*—in which questions are asked and answered in the presence of a court reporter but outside the presence of a judge

Factors that can influence the type of discovery conducted in your divorce can include:

- The types of issues in dispute
- How much access you and your spouse have to needed information
- The level of cooperation in sharing information
- The budget available for performing discovery

Talk to your attorney about the nature and extent of discovery anticipated in your case.

5.3 I thought my private postings on Facebook were safe from disclosure unless I "friended" someone? Can my Facebook postings be obtained without my consent?

We live in a society where way too much personal information is shared on the Internet. Most people would not tell a stranger half of the things that they post on the Internet. In days gone by, one would be too ashamed to "air one's dirty laundry in public." It seems now that there is some apparent pride taken in living the life of a reality TV star.

However, this information can be devastating when one is going through a divorce. More and more divorce attorneys have become experts on social media because social media can be an excellent source of incriminating and damning evidence. Many family law attorneys are routinely requesting opposing parties' social media accounts and many courts are ordering this information to be turned over. Don't think for a moment that just because you removed a posting, someone else hasn't saved it, and that person is likely not your friend.

There have been many cases where a spouse was caught cheating and the photos and messages posted to social media proved the adultery—or simply proved what a horribly mean person one party or the other appears to be. Because of the prevalence of social media and the impact that it has had on divorce cases, these are a few points that common sense suggests is a wiser course of action:

Stop posting to social media! Is it really that important to you? It is not smart to say something online and have it there forever. The reason that I advise against posting to social media is that when you do post a comment, you do it at your own risk. If you *don't* do it, then there is no chance of harming yourself. However, if you do post, make sure that anything you post is something that you would read to your grandmother or to the judge in your case. If a post would need explanation to justify its posting, then it probably should not be posted because if you must explain, it is already a problem.

Change your passwords. Most couples share at least one password and at least one account. This can be disastrous in a divorce. When you change your passwords, make sure to change them to something secure and not similar or easily guessed by anyone who knows you well. There have been many events where the other person guesses his or her partner's password. Also, be sure to change the security questions—even making up a false answer that no one would guess. Beware of BFF (so-called: "Best Friends Forever")—who have been known to turn traitor and share all your secrets with the exact person you don't want to know those matters. Such "secret" matters can be admissible into evidence.

Set all profiles to private. Double- and triple-check all of your security settings. You do not want to share something that could potentially hurt you. Make sure you "unfriend" anyone who might disclose your information. Search the Help section on Facebook to find out exactly how to do this. Oftentimes people will set their profile to "private" and forget to "unfriend" their spouse's family members, who could provide a post to negatively affect the poster's divorce case.

Cancel the shared services. Some couples even share an e-mail account (one e-mail for both). Others may use the same Internet provider customer account, which might allow both spouses to access all data. If you are divorcing, you should examine your risk and protect against it, severing accounts if necessary. A shared account is asking for trouble in a divorce case. Imagine your spouse, or ex-spouse, running up charges on your Apple ID or Amazon account. It's also one more way that one spouse can keep tabs on the other. Make sure if the account is essential to the other spouse that you give the other party notice of the proposed cancellation or coordinate so that the other's address book is backed up if desired prior to interruption of service.

Clean or "scrub" shared gadgets. Many electronic devices store passwords and important information. Many divorce cases have turned on one spouse accessing stored information. Make sure all devices have been cleaned of stored joint passwords. Do not alter the other party's info, but make sure you are not leaving any opportunity for the other party to access your information. It would be money well spent to hire a professional to ensure this is done effectively.

Secure your own devices. Hand in hand with resetting passwords, make it known that your spouse, or ex-spouse, no longer has permission to use the device. If you believe that the other party has planted a virus or spyware, then you should hire a professional to run a virus and spyware search or reset the device.

5.4   How long does the discovery process take?

Discovery can take anywhere from a few weeks to a number of months, depending upon factors such as the complexity of the case, the cooperation of you and your spouse, and whether expert witnesses are involved.

Generally, the Georgia Rules of Discovery provide that interrogatories and requests for production of documents be responded to within thirty days of receipt of the requests. However, if the requests are served with the complaint for divorce, then the Georgia Rules allow forty-five days for the responses to these requests. But be cautious of the deadlines as certain requests may require an earlier response. Discuss the specifics with your lawyer.

As a general rule in Georgia, any desired discovery procedures must be started promptly and completed without unnecessary delay within six months after the filing of the answer. However, as with any general rule, the court in its discretion may extend, reopen, or shorten the time for discovery.

5.5   My attorney insists that we conduct discovery, but I don't want to spend the time and money on it. Is it really necessary?

The discovery process can be critical to a successful outcome in your case for several reasons:

- It increases the likelihood that any agreements reached are on based upon accurate information.
- It provides necessary information for deciding whether to settle or proceed to trial.
- It supports the preparation of defenses by providing information regarding your spouse's case.
- It avoids surprises at trial, such as unexpected witness testimony.

Discuss with your attorney the intention behind the discovery being conducted in your case to ensure it is consistent with your goals and a meaningful investment of your legal fees.

If your attorney tells you that certain documents are required to adequately present your case and you are unable to get these documents on your own, then conducting discovery may be your only option. The extra money spent on discovery may be a necessary expense and may prove to be worth the cost in the long run.

Discovery is sometimes a necessary evil—it's better to have the documents or potential testimony than to not have it and go to trial and be surprised, or to find out important information later when the case is over.

Be aware also that the discovery process can be mandatory, not optional.

5.6   I just received from my spouse's attorney interrogatories and requests that I produce documents. My attorney wants me to respond within two weeks. I'll never make the deadline. What can I do?

Your attorney has requested that you provide him with the responses sooner than they are due to the other party because your attorney wants to review your responses and documents produced.

Answering your discovery promptly will help move your case forward and help control your legal fees. There are steps you can take to make this task easier.

First, look at all of the questions. Many of them will not apply or your answers will be a simple "yes" or "no."

Break it down into smaller tasks. If you answer just a few questions a day, the job will not be so overwhelming.

Call your attorney and ask whether a paralegal in the office can help you organize the needed information or determine whether some of it can be provided at a later date.

Delay in the discovery process often leads to frustration by clients and attorneys. Do your best to provide the information in a timely manner with the help of others.

For the requested documents, it is important to remember that they are documents that you have. A general rule of thumb is that if you can go online and print them then you need to do that, but if you have to go somewhere, request the documents, and pay a fee then you don't have to do that.

5.7 My spouse's attorney intends to subpoena my medical records. Aren't these private?

Whether or not your medical records are relevant in your case will depend upon the issues in dispute. If you are requesting alimony or if your health is an issue in the dispute of child custody, these records may be relevant.

Talk with your attorney about your rights. It may be that a motion to stop the subpoena, known as a *motion to quash* or a motion for a *protective order,* is needed, or that the nature of the records that can be obtained should be limited to those relevant to your divorce.

5.8 It's been two months since my attorney sent interrogatories to my spouse, and we still don't have his answers. I answered mine on time. Is there anything that can be done to speed up the process?

First, feel good about responding to your obligation in time. It is important to remember that you can control only your actions. The failure or refusal of a spouse to follow the rules of discovery can add to both the frustration and expense of the divorce process. However, you need to continue on the path that you are on—don't sink to your spouse's level. Remember: Two wrongs don't make a right!

Talk with your attorney about filing a *motion to compel,* seeking a court order that your spouse provides the requested information by a certain date. A request for attorney fees for the filing of the motion may also be appropriate.

Ask your attorney whether a subpoena of information from an employer or a financial institution would be a more cost-effective way to get needed facts and documents if your spouse remains uncooperative.

5.9 What is a *deposition*?

A *deposition* is the asking and answering of questions under oath, outside court, in the presence of a court reporter. A deposition may be taken of you, your spouse, and potential witnesses in your divorce case, including experts. Both attorneys will be present. You and your spouse also have the right to be present during the taking of depositions of any witnesses in your case.

Depositions are not performed in every divorce. They are most common in cases involving contested custody, complex financial issues, and expert witnesses.

After your deposition is completed, the questions and answers will be transcribed, that is, typed, by the court reporter exactly as given and bound into one or more volumes.

5.10   What is the purpose of a deposition?

A deposition can serve a number of purposes, such as:

- Supporting the settlement process by providing valuable information

- Helping your attorney determine who to use as witnesses at trial

- Aiding in the assessment of a witness's credibility, that is, whether the witness appears to be telling the truth

- Helping avoid surprise at trial by learning the testimony of witnesses in advance

- Preserving testimony in the event the witness becomes unavailable for trial

Depositions can be essential tools in a divorce, especially when a case is likely to proceed to trial.

5.11   Will what I say in my deposition be used against me when we go to court?

It can be. Usually, depositions are used to develop trial strategy and obtain information in preparation for trial. In some circumstances, a deposition may be used at trial.

If you are later called to testify as a witness and you give testimony contrary to your deposition, your deposition can be used to *impeach* you by showing the inconsistency in your statements. This could cause you to lose credibility with the court, rendering your testimony less valuable. It is important to review your deposition prior to your live testimony to ensure consistency and prepare yourself for the type of questions you may be asked.

If there is a particular part of your deposition that you are concerned about, then discuss that with your attorney.

5.12   Will the judge read the depositions?

Unless a witness becomes unavailable for trial or gives conflicting testimony at trial, it is unlikely that the judge will ever read the depositions.

5. 13   How should I prepare for my deposition?

To prepare for your deposition, review the important documents in your case such as the complaint, your answers to interrogatories, and your financial affidavit.

Gather all documents you've been asked to provide at your deposition. Deliver them to your attorney in advance of your deposition for copying and review. Talk to your attorney about the type of questions you can expect to be asked. The best advice is to take a step back and try to remember all the negative things your spouse has accused you of in the past and then focus on the things that you think your spouse would have told his or her attorney and try to plan responses to each of these things. Discuss with your attorney any questions you are concerned about answering.

The best advice for a deposition is to tell the truth and answer only the question that was asked.

5.14   What will I be asked in a deposition? Can I refuse to answer questions?

Questions in a deposition can cover a broad range of topics including your education, work, income, and family. The attorney is allowed to ask anything that is reasonably calculated to lead to the discovery of admissible evidence. If the question may lead to relevant information, it can be asked in a deposition, even though it may be inadmissible at trial. If you are unsure whether to answer a question, ask your attorney and follow his or her advice. However, try to discuss these issues with your attorney before the deposition because asking your attorney if you should answer a question during the deposition will draw more attention to it, and the opposing attorney may focus on the issue.

Your attorney also may object to inappropriate questions. If there is an objection, say nothing until the attorneys discuss the objection. You will be directed whether to answer.

You should discuss sensitive information with your attorney before the deposition. This way your attorney will know how to direct you if this information is requested at your deposition.

5.15   What if I give incorrect information in my deposition?

You will be under oath during your deposition, so it is very important that you be truthful. If you give incorrect information by mistake, contact your attorney as soon as you realize the error. If you lie during your deposition, you risk being impeached by the other attorney during your divorce trial. This could cause you to lose credibility with the court, rendering your testimony less valuable.

As an additional safeguard, after your deposition is concluded and the court reporter has transcribed your deposition, you will be given time to review it and to make comments or limited changes to it. This is known as the *errata sheet*. It is very important to discuss these specifics with your attorney.

5.16   What if I don't know or can't remember the answer to a question?

You may be asked questions about which you have no knowledge. It is always acceptable to say "I don't know" if you do not have the knowledge. Similarly, if you cannot remember, simply say so. It is better to respond this way than to speculate or guess.

5.17   What else do I need to know about having my deposition taken?

The following suggestions will help you to give a successful deposition:

- Prepare for your deposition by reviewing and providing necessary documents and talking with your attorney.
- Get a good night's sleep the night before the deposition. Eat a meal with protein to sustain your energy, because the length of depositions can vary.
- Arrive early for your deposition so that you have time to get comfortable with your surroundings.

- Relax. You are going to be asked questions about matters you know. Your deposition is likely to begin with routine matters such as your educational and work history.

- Tell the truth, including whether you have met with an attorney or discussed preparation for the deposition.

- Stay calm. Your spouse's attorney will be judging your credibility and demeanor. Do not argue with the attorneys.

- Listen carefully to the entire question. Do not try to anticipate questions or start thinking about your answer before the attorney has finished asking the question.

- Answer the question directly. If the question calls only for "yes" or "no," provide such an answer.

- Do not volunteer information. If the attorney wants to elicit more information, he or she will do so in following questions.

- If you do not understand the question clearly, ask that it be repeated or rephrased. Do not try to answer what you *think* was asked.

- Take your time and carefully consider the question before answering. There is no need to hurry. If you do not know or cannot remember the answer, say so. That is an adequate answer.

- Do not guess.

- If your answer is an estimate or approximation, say so. Do not let an attorney pin you down to anything you are not sure about. For example, if you cannot remember the number of times an event occurred, say that. If the attorney asks you if it was more than ten times, answer only if you can. If you can provide a range (more than ten but less than twenty) with reasonable certainty, you may do so.

- If an attorney mischaracterizes something you said earlier, say so.

- Speak clearly and loudly enough for everyone to hear you.

- Answer all questions with words rather than gestures or sounds. "Uh-huh" is difficult for the court reporter to distinguish from "unh-unh" and may result in inaccuracies in the transcript.

- If you need a break at any point in the deposition, you have a right to request one. You can talk to your attorney during such a break.

- Discuss with your attorney in advance of your deposition whether you should review the transcript of your deposition for its accuracy or whether you should waive your right to review and sign the deposition.

- Remember that the purpose of your deposition is to support a good outcome in your case. Completing it will help your case to move forward.

5.18   Are depositions always necessary? Does every witness have to be deposed?

Depositions are less likely to be needed if you and your spouse are reaching agreement on most of the facts in your case and you are moving toward a settlement. They are more likely to be needed in cases where child custody is disputed or where there are complex financial issues. Although depositions of all witnesses are usually unnecessary, it is common to take the depositions of expert witnesses.

The taking of depositions can be based on your trial strategy. This is why it is important to discuss this with your attorney. It may be in your best interest for your attorney to know what the witnesses are going to testify to before actually having them testify to the judge. It is better to be safe than to be surprised at trial.

5.19   Will I get a copy of the depositions in my case?

Ask your attorney for copies of the depositions in your case. Your attorney will have to get a copy from the court reporter and this will cost you, but it will be a small price to pay so that you are prepared for trial. It will be important for you to carefully review your deposition if your case proceeds to trial.

6

Mediation and Negotiation

Any agreement you can live with is better than trusting twelve strangers on a jury to make a sound judgment looking at the snapshot of evidence at court.
You know the whole truth, but the jury never does.

If your marriage has been difficult, you probably expect your divorce to be difficult. You picture yourself retaining a lawyer with a reputation as a "barracuda" because you have an angry spouse and there is increasing animosity between the two of you. You wonder if there is any way out of this nightmare.

Alternatively, perhaps you and your spouse are parting ways amicably. Although you don't necessarily agree on all the terms and conditions of your divorce, each of you is hopeful that the divorce will be a reasonable and respectful process. You want to spend your hard-earned money moving forward rather than paying high attorney fees, expert witness fees, and costs.

In either case, going to trial and having a judge make all of the decisions in your divorce is not inevitable. In fact, most Georgia divorce cases settle without the need for a trial.

Mediation and negotiation can help you and your spouse resolve your disputed issues without taking your case before the judge (or jury) who will make your decisions for you. You reach your own agreements rather than allow the court to make them for you.

Resolving your divorce through a mediated or negotiated settlement has many advantages. You can achieve a mutually satisfying agreement, a known outcome, little risk of appeal, and often enjoy significantly lower legal fees. Despite the circumstances that led to the end of your marriage, it might be possible for your divorce to conclude peacefully with the help of these tools.

6.1   What is the difference between *mediation* and *negotiation*?

The two processes are a lot alike and overlap. Both mediation and negotiation are methods used to help you and your spouse settle your divorce by reaching an agreement rather than going to trial and having the judge or a jury make decisions for you. *Mediation* is the term given to the formal process and *negotiation* refers to the technique that is used. These methods are sometimes referred to as *alternative dispute resolution* or *ADR*.

Mediation uses a trained mediator who is an independent, neutral third party. He or she is a skilled professional who can assist you and your spouse in the process. The mediator's goal is to facilitate a meaningful discussion between you and your spouse. The mediator will attempt to get each party to take a step back and evaluate the case from an outside perspective. You, your spouse, and each of your lawyers will usually be present at mediation.

Negotiation involves lawyers for both you and your spouse. Negotiation is the process of your lawyer and your spouse's lawyer communicating different offers of settlement to each other. In most cases, mediation is more successful than negotiation because of the mediator's contributions.

6.2   How are mediation and negotiation different from a *collaborative divorce*?

Collaborative law is a method of resolving a divorce case where both parties have a strong commitment to settling their disputes and avoiding litigation. You and your spouse each hire an attorney trained in the collaborative law process. You, your spouse, and your attorneys enter into an agreement that provides that, in the event either you or your spouse decides to take the case to court, both of you must terminate services with your collaborative attorneys and start anew.

Often, spouses in the collaborative process enlist the support of other professionals, such as an independent financial advisor or coaches, to support them through the process. Although the process may be lengthy, it enables the focus to shift away from the conflict and toward finding solutions. The attorneys become a part of the team supporting settlement rather than advocates adding to the conflict.

Talk to your attorney about whether your case would be well suited to the collaborative law process.

6.3   What is involved in the mediation process? What will I have to do and how long will it take?

The mediation process will be explained to you in detail by the mediator at the start of the mediation session. Mediation involves one or more meetings with you, your spouse, and the mediator. In most cases the attorneys will also be present.

The mediator will outline ground rules designed to ensure you will be treated respectfully and given an opportunity to be heard. In most cases you and your spouse will each be given an opportunity to make some opening remarks about what is important to you in the outcome of the divorce.

How long the process of mediation continues depends upon many of the same factors that affect how long your divorce will take. These include how many issues you and your spouse disagree about, the complexity of these issues, and the willingness of each of you to work toward an agreement.

Your case could settle after just a couple of hours or it might require a series of meetings. It is common for the mediator to clarify at the close of each session whether the parties are willing to continue with another session.

6.4   My attorney said that mediation and negotiation can reduce delays in completing my divorce. How can they do this?

When the issues in your divorce are decided by a judge instead of by you and your spouse, there are many opportunities for delay. These can include:

- Waiting for a trial date
- Having to return to court on a later, second date if your trial is not completed on the day it is scheduled
- Waiting for the judge's ruling on your case
- Attending additional court hearings after your trial to resolve disputes about the intention of your judge's rulings, issues that were overlooked, or disagreement regarding language of the decree

Each one of these events holds the possibility of delaying your divorce by days, weeks, or even months. Mediating or negotiating the terms of your divorce decree can eliminate these delays.

6.5 How can mediation and negotiation lower the costs of my divorce?

If your case is not settled by agreement, you will be going to trial. If the issues in your case are many or if they are complex, such as custody, the attorney's fees and other costs of going to trial can be tremendous.

By settling your case without going to trial, you may be able to save thousands of dollars in legal fees. Ask your attorney for a litigation budget that sets forth the potential costs of going to trial, so that you have some idea of these costs when deciding whether to settle an issue or to take it to trial before the judge.

6.6 Are there other benefits to mediating or negotiating a settlement?

Yes. A divorce resolved by a mediated or negotiated agreement can have these additional benefits:

Recognizing common goals. Mediation and negotiation allow for brainstorming between the parties and attorneys. Looking at all possible solutions, even the impractical ones, invites creative solutions to common goals. For example, suppose you and your spouse both agree that you need to pay your spouse some amount of equity for the family home you will keep, but you have no cash to make the payment. Together, you might come up with a number of options for accomplishing your goal and select the best one. Contrast this with the judge who simply orders you to pay the money without considering all of the possible options.

Addressing the unique circumstances of your situation. Rather than using a one-size-fits-all approach as a judge might do, a settlement reached by agreement allows you and your spouse to consider the unique circumstances of your situation in formulating a good outcome. For example, suppose you disagree about the parenting times for the Thanksgiving holiday. The judge might order you to alternate the holiday each year, even though you both would have preferred to have your child share the day.

Creating a safe place for communication. Mediation and negotiation give each party an opportunity to be heard. Perhaps you and your spouse have not yet had an opportunity to share directly your concerns about settlement. For example, you might be worried about how the temporary parenting time arrangement is impacting your children, but have not yet talked to your spouse about it. A mediation session or settlement conference can be a safe place for you and your spouse to communicate your concerns about your children or your finances.

Fulfilling your children's needs. You may see that your children would be better served by you and your spouse deciding their future rather than having it decided by a judge who does not know, love, and understand your children like the two of you do.

Eliminating the risk and uncertainty of trial. If a judge decides the outcome of your divorce, you give up control over the terms of the settlement. The decisions are left in the hands of the judge. If you and your spouse reach agreement, however, you have the power to eliminate the risk of an uncertain outcome.

Reducing the risk of harm to your children. If your case goes to trial, it is likely that you and your spouse will give testimony that will be upsetting to each other. As the conflict increases, the relationship between you and your spouse inevitably deteriorates. This can be harmful to your children. Contrast this with mediation or settlement negotiations, in which you open your communication and seek to reach agreement. It is not unusual for the relationship between the parents to improve as the professionals create a safe environment for re-building communication and reaching agreements in the best interest of a child.

Having the support of professionals. Having trained professionals such as mediators and lawyers to support you can help you to reach a fair settlement that you might think is impossible. These professionals have skills to help you focus on what is most important to you and shift your attention away from irrelevant facts. They understand the law and know the possible outcomes if your case goes to trial.

Lowering stress. The process of preparing for and going to court can be stressful. Your energy is going toward caring for your children, looking at your finances, and coping with the emotions of divorce. You might decide that you would be better served by settling your case rather than proceeding to trial.

Achieving closure. When you are going through a divorce, the process can feel as though it is taking an eternity. By reaching agreement, you and your spouse are better able to put the divorce behind you and move forward with your lives.

6.7   Is mediation mandatory?

Mediation is not mandatory prior to filing for divorce in Georgia. Depending upon the county in which your divorce is filed, mediation may be required before the judge will hear your case. Discuss with your attorney whether mediation will be required in your case.

6.8   What if I want to try mediation and my spouse doesn't?

Unless you live in a county in which mediation is mandatory, you can't force your spouse into mediation.

However, it is possible for one party to request an *order for mediation* from the judge. Most judges will order mediation if one party wants it. This option should be discussed with your attorney.

6.9   My spouse abused me and I am afraid to participate in mediation. Should I participate anyway?

If you have been a victim of domestic violence by your spouse, it is important that you discuss the appropriateness of mediation with your attorney. Mediation may not be a safe way for you to reach agreement. If the court in your county requires mediation, talk to your attorney about whether seeking a waiver of mediation is an appropriate option.

Any mediator should ask you whether you have been a victim of domestic violence prior to allowing mediation to proceed. This is critical for the mediator to both assess your safety and to ensure that the balance of power in the mediation process is maintained.

If you feel threatened or intimidated by your spouse but still want to proceed with mediation, talk to your attorney about him or her attending the mediation sessions with you. Request to have the mediation occur at your attorney's office, where you feel more comfortable. Also ask about mediating with your spouse being in a separate room, also known as a caucus.

If you do participate in mediation, insist that your mediator have a good understanding of the dynamics of domestic abuse and how they can impact the mediation process. Georgia has mediators who are specifically trained to handle domestic violence mediations. If you are a victim of domestic violence and you want to mediate, make sure your mediator is registered as a domestic violence mediator.

6.10   What training and credentials do mediators have?

The background of mediators varies. Some are attorneys; many come from other backgrounds such as counseling. Some mediators have received their training through the State of Georgia; others were trained out of state. Ask your attorney for help in finding a qualified mediator who has completed training in mediating family law cases. The availability of mediators also varies depending upon where you live. Regional mediation centers are located throughout Georgia. For further information on the training required, please review the Georgia Commission on Dispute Resolution's website at www.godr.org.

6.11   What types of issues can be mediated?

All of the issues in your case can be mediated. However, in advance of any mediation session, you should discuss with your attorney which issues you want to be mediated.

The local court rules in your county may require that you participate in mediation before you are able to present any issues to the judge. Talk with your attorney in advance of any mediation about custody to be absolutely clear about the impact of custody decisions on child support. Agreeing to certain custody terms can drastically reduce child support, and you should not negotiate on child custody and parenting time without having first fully discussed with your attorney its impact on child support.

You may decide that certain issues are nonnegotiable for you. Discuss this with your attorney in advance of any mediation session so that he or she can support you in focusing the discussions on the issues you are open to negotiating.

6.12 What is the role of my attorney in the mediation process?

The role of your attorney in the mediation process will vary depending upon your situation. Your attorney can be as involved (or uninvolved) as you want him or her to be. Your attorney can assist you in identifying which issues will be discussed in mediation and which are better left to the judge. Your attorney will be able to alert you of possible future issues that you may not be thinking about, and your attorney will be able to discuss the enforceability of an agreement, if one is reached.

If you have minor children, it is essential that you discuss with your attorney how sharing physical custody of your children can significantly lower child support. In all cases it is important that your attorney review any agreements discussed in mediation before a final agreement is reached.

6.13 How do I prepare for mediation?

Prior to attending a mediation session with your spouse, discuss with your attorney the issues you intend to mediate and the potential impact your decisions might have in the future. Enlist your attorney's support in identifying your intentions for the mediation. Make a list of the issues most important to you. For example, when it comes to your child, you might consider whether it is your child's safety, the parenting time schedule, or the ability to attend your children's events that concerns you more.

It is important to think about the future. You should think about how any agreement will affect you, your spouse, your children, and others in the future. Giving thought to your desired outcomes while approaching mediation with an open mind and heart is the best way to move closer to settlement.

6.14 Do children attend the mediation sessions?

In most cases your child will not participate in the mediation. However, your case might be an exception if you have an older child who is sufficiently mature to participate in the process.

If you think your child should be at the mediation table, talk to your attorney and your mediator about the potential risks and benefits of including your child in the process.

6.15 I want my attorney to look over the agreements my spouse and I discussed in mediation before I give my final approval. Is this possible?

Definitely. Before giving your written or final approval to any agreements reached in mediation, it is critical that your attorney review the agreements first. This is necessary to ensure that you understand the terms of the settlement and its implications. Your attorney will also review the agreement for compliance with Georgia law.

Some mediators prefer to have a signed agreement before mediation is concluded. This is why it is important to have your attorney present at mediation. If your attorney is not at your mediation and you agree to something and then your attorney advises you differently, you may have wasted a day at mediation, or, worse, you may not be able to get out of your agreement.

6.16 Who pays for mediation?

The cost of mediation must be paid for by you or your spouse. Often it is a shared expense. Expect your mediator to address the matter of fees before or at your first session. Some localities have mediation centers where mediators charge reduced fees. Other places, or if the parties choose, may have private mediators who charge hourly or flat fees that are similar to your attorney fees.

6.17   What if mediation fails?

If mediation is not successful, you still may be able to settle your case through negotiations between the attorneys. Also, you and your spouse can agree to preserve the settlements that were reached and to take only the remaining disputed issues to the judge for trial. Numerous divorce cases will settle prior to trial even though they were not settled at mediation. The mediation session may have laid the framework for the eventual settlement—this is another benefit of mediation.

6.18   What is a *settlement conference*?

A *settlement conference* can be a powerful tool for the resolution of your case. It is a meeting held with you, your spouse, and your attorneys with the intention of negotiating the terms of your divorce. In some cases, a professional with important information needed to support the settlement process, such as an accountant, may also participate.

Settlement conferences are most effective when both parties and their attorneys see the potential for a negotiated resolution and have the necessary information to accomplish that goal. In some jurisdictions it may be possible to have the judge present and lead a settlement conference.

6.19   Why should I consider a settlement conference when the attorneys can negotiate through letters and phone calls?

A settlement conference can eliminate the delays that often occur when negotiation takes place through correspondence and calls between the attorneys. Rather than waiting days or weeks for a response, you can receive a response on a proposal in a matter of minutes.

A settlement conference also enables you and your spouse, if you choose, to use your own words to explain the reasoning behind your requests. You are also able to provide information immediately to expedite the process. In some cases, it is the face-to-face contact between the parties that is all it takes to settle a case. These cases allow each party to see how their respective positions and decisions are affecting the other party. Remember, you married the other party—presumably you loved him or her at some point.

6.20   How do I prepare for my settlement conference?

Being well prepared for the settlement conference can help you make the most of this opportunity to resolve your case without the need to go to trial. Actions you should take include:

- Provide all necessary information in advance of the conference. If your attorney has asked for a current pay stub, tax return, debt amounts, asset values, or other documentation, make sure it is provided prior to the meeting.

- Discuss your topics of concern with your attorney in advance. Your attorney can assist you in understanding your rights under the law so that you can have realistic expectations for the outcome of negotiations.

- Take a positive attitude, a listening ear, and an open mind. Come with the attitude that your case will settle. Be willing to first listen to the opposing party, and then to share your position. To encourage your spouse to listen to your position, listen to hers or his first. Resist the urge to interrupt.

Few cases settle without each side demonstrating flexibility and a willingness to compromise. Most cases settle when the parties are able to take these qualities to the process.

6.21   What will happen at my settlement conference?

Typically, the conference will be held at the office of one of the attorneys, with both parties and attorneys present. If there are a number of issues to be discussed, an agenda may be used to keep the focus on relevant topics. From time to time throughout the conference, you and your attorney may meet alone to consult as needed. If additional information is needed to reach agreement, some issues may be set aside for later discussion.

The length of the conference depends upon the number of issues to be resolved, the complexity of the issues, and the willingness of the parties and lawyers to communicate effectively. An effort is made to confirm which issues are resolved and which issues remain disputed. Then, one by one, the issues are addressed.

6.22 What is the role of my attorney in the settlement conference?

Your attorney is your advocate during the settlement conference. You can count on him or her to support you throughout the process, to see that important issues are addressed, and to counsel you privately outside the presence of your spouse and his or her attorney.

6.23 Why is my attorney appearing so friendly with my spouse and her attorney?

Successful negotiations rely upon building trust between the parties working toward agreement. Your attorney may be respectful or pleasant toward your spouse or your spouse's attorney to promote a good outcome for you.

The old saying "You get more bees with sugar than vinegar" comes to mind. Remember, your attorney will probably work against your spouse's attorney again. In smaller communities attorneys socialize often. But this does not mean that your attorney will not seek what is in your best interest. Your attorney took an oath to represent your best interest.

6.24 What happens if my spouse and I settled some but not all of the issues in our divorce?

You and your spouse can agree to maintain the agreements you have reached and let the judge decide those matters that you are unable to resolve.

6.25 If my spouse and I reach an agreement, how long will it take before we can go before the judge to have it approved at a final hearing?

If a settlement is reached through mediation, one of the attorneys will put the agreement in writing for approval by you and your spouse. In most cases, a final hearing is held within thirty days of the agreement being signed. Sometimes this can be sooner or longer depending on the judge's schedule. This final hearing is where one party goes before the judge and "proves the divorce." One party will tell the judge that he or she want the divorce and would like the judge to grant the divorce based on the terms of your agreement.

7

Emergency:
When You Fear Your Spouse

There is a difference between fear and worry.
Real fear requires action for protection.
Mere worry robs you of enjoying today, out of concern
for what might happen tomorrow.

Suddenly, you are in a panic. Maybe your spouse was serious when he said he'd take your child and leave the state. What if you're kicked out of your own home? Suppose all of the bank accounts are emptied? Your fear heightens as your mind spins with all of the possibilities from every horror story you have ever heard about divorce.

Facing an emergency situation in divorce can feel as though your entire life is at stake. You may not be able to concentrate on anything else. At the same time, you may be paralyzed with anxiety and have no idea how to begin to protect yourself. No doubt you have countless worries about what your future holds.

Remember that you have overcome many challenges in your life before this moment. There are people willing to help you. You have strength and wisdom you may not yet even realize. Step by step, you will make it through this time.

When facing an emergency, do your best to focus on what to do in the immediate moment. Set aside your worries about the future for another day. Now it is time to stay in the present moment, let others support you, and start taking action right away.

If physical harm is a genuine concern and serious risk, take action. Contact your local safe shelter and consider seeking without delay a court's protective order.

7.1 My spouse has deserted me, and I need to get divorced as quickly as possible. What is my first step?

Your first step is to get legal advice as soon as possible. The earlier you get legal counsel to advise you about your rights, the better. The initial consultation will answer most of your questions and start you on an action plan for getting your divorce underway.

Georgia allows for a divorce to be granted based on desertion grounds, but the statute specifies that the spouse has to be gone for twelve months or more. This does not mean that you have to wait twelve months before filing the divorce. You can always file on the grounds that the marriage is irretrievably broken, Georgia's no-fault ground.

7.2 I'm afraid my abusive spouse will try to hurt me and/or our children if I say I want a divorce. What can I do legally to protect myself and my children?

Develop a plan with your safety and that of your children as your highest priority. In addition to meeting with an attorney at your first opportunity, develop a safety plan in the event you and your children need to escape your home. A great way to do this is to let in support from an agency that helps victims of domestic violence.

Your risk of harm from an abusive spouse increases when you leave. For this reason, all actions must be taken with safety as the first concern.

Find an attorney who understands domestic violence. Often, your local domestic violence agency can help with a referral. Talk to your attorney about the concerns for your safety and that of your children. Ask your attorney about a protection order (or an *ex parte* restraining order). This is a court order that may offer a number of protections including granting you temporary custody of your children and ordering your spouse to leave the family residence and have no contact with you.

7.3   I am afraid to meet with an attorney because I am terrified my spouse will find out and get violent. What should I do?

Schedule an initial consultation with an attorney who is experienced in working with domestic violence victims. When you schedule the appointment, let the firm know your situation and instruct the law office not to place any calls that you think your spouse might discover.

Consultations with your attorney are confidential. Your attorney has an ethical duty to not disclose your meeting with anyone outside the law firm. Let your attorney know your concerns so that extra precautions can be taken by the law office in handling your file.

Make sure to discuss having your attorney request a protection order (or an *ex parte* restraining order) at the time of filing your divorce.

7.4   I want to give my attorney all the information needed so my children and I are safe from my spouse. What does this include?

Provide your attorney with complete information about the history, background, nature, and evidence of your abuse, including:

- The types of abuse (for example, physical, sexual, verbal, financial, mental, or emotional)
- The dates, time frames, or occasions
- The locations
- Whether you were ever treated medically
- Any police reports made
- E-mails, letters, notes, or journal entries
- Any photographs taken
- Any witnesses to the abuse or evidence of the abuse
- Any statements made by your spouse admitting the abuse
- Any damaged property
- Injuries you or your children suffered
- Any counseling you had because of the abuse

- Alcohol or drug abuse by your spouse
- The presence of guns or other weapons

The more detailed the information you provide to your attorney, the easier it will be for him or her to make a strong case for the protection of you and your children.

7.5   I'm not ready to hire an attorney for a divorce, but I am afraid my spouse is going to get violent with my children and me in the meantime. What can I do?

It is possible, although not recommended, to seek a protection order from the court without an attorney. It is possible for the judge to order your spouse out of your home, grant you custody of your children, and order your spouse to stay away from you.

It is also possible to contact an attorney and try to get them to help you prepare a protection order. Discuss with an attorney the possibility of him or her representing you on a limited basis. Georgia Legal Aid may be able to help prepare a protection order under these circumstances.

7.6   What's the difference between a *protection order* and a *restraining order*?

Protection orders and restraining orders are both court orders directing a person to not engage in certain behavior. Both of them are intended to protect others. Although either can initially be obtained without notice to the other person, there is always a right to a hearing to determine whether a protection order or restraining order should remain in place.

Talk to your attorney about obtaining a *protection order* if you are concerned about the safety of your children or yourself or if there has been a history of domestic violence. The violation of a protection order is a criminal offense that can result in immediate arrest.

The proper name for a protection order is a *family violence protective order*. The procedures and the grounds for having the judge grant one of these orders are laid out in the Georgia code. A family violence protective order is usually more intensive and more detailed than a restraining order. Additionally, only certain acts will qualify as grounds for getting a family violence protective order.

If you are concerned that your spouse will annoy, threaten, harass, or intimidate you after your divorce complaint is filed, ask your attorney about a restraining order. If your spouse violates the restraining order, he or she may be brought before the court for contempt.

7.7 My spouse has never been violent, but I fear it is possible there will be great anger when the divorce papers are served. Do I need a protection order?

The facts of your case may not warrant a protection order. However, if you are still concerned about your spouse's behavior, ask your attorney about a *temporary restraining order (TRO)* to be delivered to your spouse at the same time as the divorce complaint. This court order directs your spouse not to annoy, threaten, intimidate, or harass you while the divorce is in progress. A temporary restraining order can also order your spouse not to sell or transfer assets until your divorce is completed.

7.8 My spouse says I am crazy, that I am a liar, and that no judge will ever believe me if I tell the truth about the abusive behavior. What can I do if I don't have any proof?

Most domestic violence is not witnessed by third parties. Often there is little physical evidence. Even without physical evidence, a judge can enter orders to protect you and your children if you give truthful testimony about your abuse that the judge finds believable. Your own testimony of your abuse is evidence.

It is very common for persons who abuse others to claim that their victims are liars and to make statements intended to discourage disclosure of the abuse. This is yet another form of controlling behavior.

Your attorney's skills and experience will support you to give effective testimony in the courtroom to establish your case. Let your attorney know your concerns so that a strong case can be presented to the judge based upon your persuasive statements of the truth of your experience.

If you are in this type of situation, then it is important to hire an attorney who is familiar with domestic violence and knows how to handle these types of cases.

7.9 I'm afraid my spouse is going to take all of the money out of the bank accounts and leave me with nothing. What can I do?

Talk to your attorney immediately. If you are worried about your spouse emptying financial accounts or selling marital assets, it is critical that you take action at once. Your attorney can advise on your right to take possession of certain assets in order to protect them from being hidden or spent by your spouse.

Ask your attorney about seeking a temporary restraining order as to property prior to giving your spouse notice that you are filing for divorce. This order forbids your spouse to sell, transfer, hide, or otherwise dispose of marital property until the divorce is complete.

A temporary restraining order is intended to prevent assets from "disappearing" before a final division of the property from your marriage is complete.

7.10 My spouse told me that if I ever file for divorce, I'll never see my child again. Should I be worried about my child being abducted?

Your fear that your spouse will abduct your children is a common one. It can be helpful to look at some of the factors that appear to increase the risk that your child will be removed from the state by the other parent.

Most abductions are made by men. They are often from marriages that cross culture, race, religion, or ethnicity. A lower socioeconomic status, prior criminal record, and limited social or economic ties to the community can also increase risk.

Programming and brainwashing are almost always present in cases where a child is at risk for being kidnapped by a parent, and efforts to isolate the child may also be seen. Exit activities such as obtaining a new passport, getting financial matters in order, or contacting a moving company could be indicators.

Talk to your attorney to assess the risks in your particular case. Together you can determine whether statements by your spouse are threats intended to control or intimidate you or whether legal action is needed to protect your child.

To learn more about what precautions to take and what to do if something happens, visit the National Center for Missing and Exploited Children at their website at: www.missingkids.com/LegalResources/Domestic.

7.11 What legal steps can be taken to prevent my spouse from removing our child from the state?

If you are concerned about your child being removed from the state, talk to your attorney about whether any of these options might be available in your case:

- A court order giving you immediate custody until a temporary custody hearing can be held
- A court order that forbids either party from taking the minor child out of the jurisdiction of the court (basically an order restricting where the child can travel to)
- A court order directing your spouse to turn over passports for the child and your spouse to the court
- The posting of a bond prior to your spouse exercising parenting time
- Supervised visitation

Both state and federal laws are designed to provide protection from the removal of children from one state to another when a custody matter is brought and to protect children from kidnapping. *The Uniform Child Custody Jurisdiction and Enforcement Act (UCCJEA)* was passed to encourage the custody of children to be decided in the state where they have been living most recently and where they have the most ties. *The Parental Kidnapping Prevention Act (PKPA)* makes it a federal crime for a parent to kidnap a child in violation of a valid custody order.

If you are concerned about your child being abducted, talk with your attorney about all the options available to you for your child's protection.

If abduction is a possibility, then remember that an order from the court is a piece of paper that has to be enforced. If this is an area that really concerns you then, you should take a look at the National Center for Missing and Exploited Children's website at www.missingkids.com/home. This website contains helpful information on prevention and what to do if something does happen.

7.12   How quickly can I get a divorce in Georgia?

There are a number of time requirements for getting a divorce in Georgia. Either you or your spouse must have been a resident of Georgia for at least six months prior to the filing of the complaint for the divorce with the court. After you file your divorce, your spouse must be given notice of the divorce.

A forty-five-day waiting period is required for every Georgia divorce. This period begins on either the date the sheriff serves your spouse with the divorce complaint or the date that a voluntary appearance signed by your spouse is filed with the court.

The earliest a final hearing can be held is thirty-one days after service or acknowledgment of service, but this requires a waiver to be signed by both parties. Most cases do not resolve this quickly. The length of time your case remains pending depends in large part upon the extent to which you and your spouse reach agreement on the issues in your case.

Once a final hearing or trial is held and the judge signs your divorce decree, it becomes final.

7.13   I really need a divorce quickly. Will the divorce I get in another country be valid in Georgia?

If both you and your spouse consider Georgia as your true home and you both intend to remain in the state, a divorce from another state or country will more than likely not be valid. If Georgia is the permanent home for both of you, it would be difficult to obtain a divorce in another state or country, even if you reside there temporarily and, even if you did get the divorce, the chances of it being enforced in Georgia are not good.

These are important issues that should be addressed with your attorney. Oftentimes divorces from other countries, where you do not live and do not have any ties, are a sham. These divorces are usually a waste of money and are not recognized by the state of Georgia.

7.14   If either my spouse or I file for divorce, will I be ordered out of my home? Who decides who gets to live in the house while we go through the divorce?

If you and your spouse cannot reach agreement regarding which of you will leave the residence during the divorce, the judge will decide whether one of you should be granted exclusive possession of the home until the case is concluded. In some cases judges have been known to refuse to order either party out of the house until the divorce is concluded or at least until a temporary hearing can be held where both parties have a chance to present their evidence.

Abusive behavior is one basis for seeking temporary possession of the home. If there are minor children, the custodial parent will ordinarily be awarded temporary possession of the residence.

Other factors the judge may consider include:

- Whether one of you owned the home prior to the marriage

- After provisions are made for payment of temporary support, who can afford to remain in the home or obtain other housing

- Who is most likely to be awarded the home in the divorce

- Options available to each of you for temporary housing, including other homes or family members who live in the area

- Special needs that would make a move unduly burdensome, such as a health condition

- Self-employment from home, which could not be readily moved, such as a child-care business

If staying in the home is important to you, talk to your attorney about your reasons so that a strong case can be made for you at the temporary hearing.

8

Child Custody

If circumstances preclude your child being raised in a two-parent home, then strive to put your child first,
at least until eighteen years of age.
Make life choices consistent with the best interest of your child.
When you share your child, do your part to provide that child
with two sane parents existing in a healthful,
peaceful environment.

Your children, progeny, offspring, young'uns—they're your lasting legacy to the world. Ever since you and your spouse began talking (or thinking) about divorce, chances are your progeny, whom you both love, may have been the greatest concern of one or both of you.

The decision to seek divorce might have even been delayed because of concern about the impact on your mutual offspring. Now that the time has come, it is natural that you have serious concerns about divorce's impact on your children. Will they be scarred for life? Will they blame themselves? Will they still love you after their world changes and they live somewhere they might not want?

Ask yourself these questions: Have you been making wise and loving decisions for your children since they were born? Have you always put their best interest ahead of yours? Have you always done your best to see that they had everything they really needed? Have you loved them, nurtured them, and protected them? Realize that this won't change simply because you are going through a divorce. If you were a good parent before the divorce, you can still be a good parent after the divorce.

It can be difficult not to worry about how sharing parenting time with the other parent will affect your children, and you as well. You may also have fears about being cut out of your children's lives. Try to remember that, regardless of who has custody, it is likely that the court order will not only give you a lot of time with your children but also a generous opportunity to be involved in their day-to-day lives.

With the help of your attorney, you can make sound decisions regarding the custody arrangement that is in the best interest of each child and will maintain the loving bond you want.

8.1   What types of custody are awarded in Georgia?

Under Georgia law, there are two aspects to a custody determination. These are *legal custody* and *physical custody*. *Legal custody* refers to the power to make important decisions regarding your children. Legal custody may be awarded to you, to your spouse, or to both of you jointly (and in some limited cases to a third party).

The parent with legal custody is the primary and final decision maker for significant matters regarding the child, such as which school the child attends and who will be the child's health-care providers. The noncustodial parent will have parenting time and other rights.

Joint legal custody means both parents share equally in the decision making for the child. If joint legal custody is awarded, then the court will require that, for the times when parents do not agree, a tie-breaking mechanism be in place. Giving one parent final say avoids the delay, stress, and cost of every disagreement having to go back to court for the judge to decide on matters of education, health, extracurricular activities, and other important matters, when the parents cannot agree after a good-faith discussion.

The tie-breaking authority may be given to the primary physical custodian of the child, or the authority could be divided between the parents on different issues. Mom might get final say on education and medical. Dad might get final say on extracurricular and religious issues. The final decision power might even be left up to a third party such as a grandmother. If you and the other parent are unable to reach agreement, you may need to seek resolution through mediation or return to court to get the issue resolved.

Joint legal custody is often favored in Georgia. But, for joint legal custody to work, certain factors have to be present—the same factors that, if missing, may be contributing to the need for divorce, such as:

- Effective and open communication between the parents concerning the child
- A strong desire on the part of both parents to continue to be a parenting team, to co-parent together
- A history of active involvement of both parents in the child's life
- Similar parenting values held by both parents
- A willingness on the part of both parents to place the child's needs before their own
- Both parents' willingness to be flexible and compromising about making decisions concerning the child

Physical custody refers to the where and with whom the children spend the majority of their time. Like legal custody, it may be awarded to either parent or to both parents jointly (or in limited cases to a third party). Joint physical custody is sometimes referred to as *shared physical custody.*

Specified parenting time is usually awarded to each parent, regardless of who has physical custody. Provisions for days of the week, school breaks, summer, holidays, birthdays, and vacations are typically provided for in detail. In the event that one of your children will reside with you and another child will reside with the other *parent, the arrangement is referred to as* split physical custody.

If you are considering joint custody, be sure to discuss with your attorney not only the best interest of your child, but also the possible ramifications on paying or receiving child support resulting from the custody decision. An award of joint (shared) physical custody can result in a substantial reduction in child support.

8.2 On what basis will the judge make the decision on custody?

Georgia law says that there is no presumption for the custody of the child for either the mother or the father. This means that, generally, at the start of your case, the mother and the father are on equal footing regarding custody. The judge may take into consideration all the circumstances of the case and will have to consider many factors when trying to determine child custody. Although many factors may be considered, the overarching standard is: What is in the best interest of the child to best promote the child's welfare and happiness? The decision on custody will be made solely by the judge. The law requires the judge to exercise sound discretion and make a decision based on the evidence presented.

The judge may look at any relevant factor, but the factors described following are the most common:

- The love, affection, bonding, and emotional ties existing between each parent and the child
- The love, affection, bonding, and emotional ties existing between the child and siblings, half-siblings, and step-siblings and the residence of such other children
- The capacity and disposition of each parent to give the child love, affection, and guidance and to continue the education and rearing of the child (The emotional relationship between your child and each parent may include the nature of the bond between the parent and child and the feelings shared between the child and each parent.)
- Each parent's knowledge and familiarity of the child and the child's needs
- The capacity and disposition of each parent to provide the child with food, clothing, medical care, day-to-day needs, and other necessary basic care, with consideration made for the potential payment of child support by the other parent (Here the court may examine whether you or the other parent is better able to provide for your child's daily needs such as nutrition, health care, hygiene, social activities, nurturing, and education. The court may also look to see whether

you or the other parent have been attending to these needs in the past.)

- The home environment of each parent considering the promotion of nurturance and safety of the child rather than superficial or material factors (This refers to the respective environments offered by you and the other parent. The court may consider factors such as the safety, stability, and nurturing found in each home.)
- The importance of continuity in the child's life and the length of time the child has lived in a stable, satisfactory environment and the desirability of maintaining continuity (This factor might be applied in your case if you stayed at home for a period of years to care for your child, and awarding custody to the other parent would disrupt your relationship with your child.)
- The stability of the family unit of each of the parents and the presence or absence of each parent's support systems within the community to benefit the child
- The mental and physical health of each parent
- Each parent's involvement, or lack thereof, in the child's educational, social, and extracurricular activities
- Each parent's employment schedule and the related flexibility or limitations, if any, of a parent to care for the child
- The home, school, and community record and history of the child, as well as any health or educational special needs of the child (Every child is unique. Your child's needs must be considered when it comes to deciding custody and parenting time. The custody of a child with special needs, for example, may be awarded to the parent who is better able to meet those needs.)
- Whether you or the other parent has fulfilled the role of primary care provider for meeting the day-to-day needs of your child

- Each parent's past performance and relative abilities for future performance of parenting responsibilities (Georgia does not follow the "tender years" doctrine, which formerly gave a preference for custody of very young children to the mother.) If one of the parents has an illness that may impair the ability to parent, it may be considered by the court.

- The willingness and ability of each of the parents to facilitate and encourage a close and continuing parent-child relationship between the child and the other parent, consistent with the best interest of the child

- Any recommendation by a court-appointed custody evaluator or guardian *ad litem*

- Any evidence of family violence or sexual, mental, or physical child abuse or criminal history of either parent (Domestic violence is an important factor in determining custody, as well as parenting time and protection from abuse during the transfer of your child to the other parent. If domestic violence is a concern in your case, be sure to discuss it in detail with your attorney during the initial consultation so that every measure can be taken to protect the safety of you and your children.)

- Any evidence of substance abuse by either parent

8.3   What's the difference between *visitation* and *parenting time*?

Historically, time spent with the noncustodial parent was referred to as *visitation*. Today, the term *parenting time* is used to refer to the time a child spends with either parent.

This change in language reflects the intention that children spend time with both parents and have two homes, as opposed to their living with one parent and visiting the other. However, the terms are sometimes still used interchangeably and can mean the same thing depending on your attorney and the judge.

8.4 How can I make sure I will get to keep the children during the divorce proceedings?

A temporary court order is the best way to be sure your children will stay with you while your divorce is proceeding. Even if you and the other parent have agreed to temporary arrangements, talk with your attorney about whether this agreement should be formalized in a court order so that it can be enforced.

Obtaining a temporary order can be an important protection not only for the custody of your children, but for other issues such as support and temporary exclusive possession of the marital home.

Until a temporary order is entered, it's best that you continue to reside with your children if obtaining custody of them is important to you. It is usually recommended that the children stay in the family home. If you must leave your home, take your children with you and talk with your attorney about seeking the appropriate court orders. These might include orders for temporary protection, custody, support, possession of your home, or attorney fees.

8.5 How can I prove that I was the primary care provider?

One tool to assist you and your attorney in establishing your case as a primary care provider is a chart indicating the care you and the other parent have each provided for your child. The clearer you are about the history of parenting, the better job your attorney can do in presenting your case to the judge.

Look at the activities in the Parental Roles Chart, below, to help you review the role of you and the other parent as care providers for your child.

Parental Roles Chart

Activity	Mother	Father
Attended prenatal medical visits		
Attended prenatal class		
Took time off work after child was born		
Got up with child for feedings		

Parental Roles Chart (Continued)

Activity	Mother	Father
Got up with child when sick at night		
Bathed child		
Put child to sleep		
Potty-trained child		
Prepared and fed meals to child		
Helped child learn numbers, letters, colors		
Helped child with practice for sports, dance, music		
Took time off work for child's appointments		
Stayed home from work with sick child		
Took child to doctor visits		
Went to pharmacy for child's medication		
Administered child's medication		
Took child to therapy		
Took child to optometrist		
Took child to dentist		
Took child to get haircuts		
Bought clothing for child		
Bought school supplies for child		
Transported child to school		
Picked child up after school		
Drove carpool for child's school		
Went to child's school activities		
Helped child with homework and projects		
Attended parent-teacher conferences		
Helped in child's classroom		
Chaperoned child's school trips and activities		

Parental Roles Chart (Continued)

Activity	Mother	Father
Transported child to day care		
Communicated with day-care providers		
Transported child from day care		
Attended day-care activities		
Signed child up for sports, dance, music		
Attended sports, music, dance practices		
Attended sports, music, dance recitals		
Coached child's sports		
Transported child from sports, music, dance		
Knows child's friends and friends' families		
Took child to religious education		
Participated in child's religious education		
Obtained information and training about special needs of child		
Comforted child during times of emotional upset		

8.6   Do I have to let my spouse see the children before we are actually divorced?

Georgia law states that "it is the express policy of this state to encourage that a child has continuing contact with parents and grandparents who have shown the ability to act in the best interest of the child and to encourage parents to share in the rights and responsibilities of raising their child after such parents have separated or dissolved their marriage or relationship."

Unless your children are at risk for being harmed by the other parent, your children should maintain regular contact with the other parent.

It is important for children to experience the presence of both parents in their lives, regardless of the separation of the parents. Even if there is no temporary order for parenting time, cooperate with the other parent in making reasonable arrangements for time with your children.

When safety is not an issue, if you deny contact with the other parent prior to trial, your judge is likely to question whether you have the best interest of your child at heart. Talk to the other parent or your attorney about what parenting time schedule would be best for your children on a temporary basis.

8.7   I am seeing a therapist. Will that hurt my chances of getting custody?

If you are seeing a therapist, acknowledge yourself for getting the professional support you need. Your well-being is important to your ability to be the best parent you can be.

Talk to your attorney about the possible implications, if any, of your being treated by a therapist. It may be that the condition for which you are being treated in no way affects your child or your ability to be a loving and supportive parent.

Your mental health records may be subpoenaed by the other parent's lawyer. For this reason it is important to discuss with your attorney an action plan for responding to a request to obtain records in your therapist's file. Ask your attorney to contact your therapist to alert him or her regarding how to respond to a request for your mental health records.

8.8   Can having a live-in partner hurt my chances of getting custody?

More often than not the answer is "yes," but each case is different. If you are contemplating having your partner live with you, discuss your decision with your attorney first. If you are already living with your partner, let your attorney know right away so that the potential impact on any custody ruling can be assessed.

Your intimate living with someone who is not your spouse may have significant impact on your custody case. However, judges' opinions of the significance of this factor can vary greatly. Talk promptly and frankly with your attorney. It will be important for you to look together at many aspects, including the following:

- How the judge assigned to your case views this situation

- Whether your living arrangement is likely to prompt a custody dispute that would otherwise not arise
- How long you have been separated from the other parent
- How long you have been in a relationship with your new partner
- The history and nature of the children's relationship with your partner
- Your future plans with your partner (such as marriage)
- Your new partner's character and past history

Living with a partner may put your custody case at risk. Think carefully before making such a decision, considering the advice of your attorney.

8.9 Will all the sordid details of my or my spouse's affair have to come out in court in front of our children?

Judges make every effort to protect children from the conflict of their parents. For this reason, most judges will not allow children to be present in the courtroom to hear the testimony of other witnesses.

Although the risk that the other parent may share information with your child cannot be eliminated, it would be highly unusual for a judge to allow a child to hear such testimony in a courtroom. If you believe that the other parent is discussing the details of your case with your children, then you should bring this to your attorney's attention immediately. Judges will typically take measures to prevent this conduct.

8.10 Should I hire a private detective to prove my spouse is having an affair?

It depends. If custody is disputed and the other parent is having an affair, discuss with your attorney how a private investigator might help you gather evidence to support your case. Discuss the following considerations with your attorney:

- What view on extramarital relationships does the judge hold?
- How is the affair affecting the children?
- How much will a private investigator cost?
- Will the evidence gathered help my case?

Your attorney can help you determine whether hiring a private investigator is a good idea in your particular case. Oftentimes the decision to hire a private investigator comes down to a cost-benefit analysis—meaning how much the private investigator is going to cost versus how much evidence he may come up with and how beneficial that evidence is going to be.

8.11 Will the fact that I had an affair during the marriage hurt my chances of getting custody?

Whether a past affair will have any impact on your custody case will depend upon many factors, including:

- The views of the judge assigned to your case
- Whether the affair had any impact on the children
- How long ago the affair occurred
- The quality of the evidence about the affair
- To some extent the details of the affair and about the other individual

If you had an affair during your marriage, discuss it with your attorney at the outset so that you can discuss its impact, if any, on custody.

8.12 During the months it takes to get a divorce, is it okay to date or will it hurt my chances at custody?

The general answer is do not date. You are still married until the final order is signed by the judge. So, why take the chances—you have enough to be concerned about already; don't add to it.

If custody is disputed, talk with your attorney about your plans to begin dating. Your dating may be irrelevant if the children are unaware of it. However, most judges will frown upon exposing your children to a new relationship when they are still adjusting to the separation of their parents.

If the other parent is contesting custody, you may decide that it would be best to focus your energy on your children, the litigation, and taking care of yourself.

If you do date and become sexually involved with your new partner, it is imperative that your children not be exposed to any sexual activity. If they are, it could harm your case for custody.

8.13 I'm gay and came out to my spouse when I filed for divorce. What impact will my sexual orientation have on my case for custody or parenting time?

There are no laws in Georgia that limit your rights as a parent based upon your sexual orientation. Social science research shows that gay and lesbian parents are more similar than dissimilar to heterosexual parents.

Exposing your child to sexual activity or engaging in sexual activity that harms your child are relevant factors in a custody dispute. However, your sexual orientation is not the same thing as your sexual activity. Be aware that regardless of your sexual orientation, judges don't generally like new partners being introduced to the children during a divorce case. The children already have a lot going on and introducing your new partner to them may not be in their best interest.

Be sure to choose an attorney whom you have confidence will fully support you in your goals as a parent. Understand that, to dispel certain myths (such as: "being homosexual or lesbian means that person is also sexually attracted to children as a pedophile"), the other parent may need to be educated, along with opposing counsel, and possibly even the judge.

8.14 How is *abandonment* legally defined, and how might it affect the outcome of our custody battle?

Abandonment is rarely an issue in custody litigation unless one parent has been absent from the child's life for an extended period.

Under Georgia law, abandonment is determined by the facts and circumstances of each case. There is no magic time frame for someone's absence (however, one year is typically used). Abandonment has to be proven by clear and convincing evidence, and it has to be shown that the parent had the intention to sever the parental relationship, and thereby avoid all of the obligations of being a parent. Georgia also describes this as the failure to provide the necessities of life. The intentional absence of a parent's presence, care, protection, and support are all considered.

If you believe that the other parent has abandoned his or her rights to custody, then discuss your facts with your lawyer.

8.15 Can I have witnesses speak on my behalf to try to get custody of my children?

Absolutely. Witnesses are critical in every custody case. At a temporary hearing, a witness is more likely to provide testimony by affidavit, which is a written, sworn statement. However, at a trial for the final determination of custody, you and the other parent will each have an opportunity to have witnesses give live testimony on your behalf.

Among those you might consider as potential witnesses in your custody case are:

- Family members
- Family friends
- Child-care providers
- Neighbors
- Teachers
- Health-care providers
- Clergy members

In considering which witnesses would best support your case, your attorney may consider the following:

- What has been this witness's opportunity to observe you or the other parent, especially with your child. How frequently? How recently?
- How long has the witness known you or the other parent?
- What is the relationship of the witness to the child and the parents?
- How valuable is the knowledge that this witness has?
- Does this witness have knowledge different from that of other witnesses?
- Is the witness available and willing to testify?
- Is the witness clear in conveying information?
- Is the witness credible, that is, will the judge believe this witness?
- Does the witness have any biases or prejudices that could impact the testimony?

You and your attorney can work together to determine which witnesses will best support your case. Support your attorney by providing a list of potential witnesses together with your opinion regarding the answers to the above questions.

Give your attorney the phone numbers, addresses, and workplaces of each of your potential witnesses. This information can be critical for the role that the attorney has in interviewing the witnesses, contacting them regarding testifying, and issuing subpoenas to compel their court attendance if needed. When parents give conflicting testimony during a custody trial, the testimony of other witnesses can be key to determining the outcome of the case. Judges generally focus on witnesses who are not biased and have no stake in the outcome of the decision.

8.16   How much weight does the child's preference carry?

The preference of your child is only one of many factors a judge considers in determining custody. In Georgia, once a child has reached the age of fourteen, the child will have the right to select which parent he or she wants to live with. The child's selection is presumptive unless the court determines that the parent selected is not in the child's best interest. If your child is between the ages of eleven and fourteen, then the judge will consider your child's selection, but the judge shall have complete discretion in making the determination of what is in your child's best interest, and the child's desires shall not be controlling.

Consider the thirteen-year-old girl who wants to live with her mother because "Mom lets me stay out past curfew, I get a bigger allowance, and I don't have to do chores." This preference is not likely to be approved by the judge. Of course, more likely approval would be given to the preference of a eleven-year-old who wants to live with his mother because "she helps me with my homework, reads me bedtime stories, and doesn't call me names like Dad does."

If you see that your child's preference may be a factor in the determination of custody, discuss it with your attorney so that this consideration is a part of assessing the action to be taken in your case.

8.17 How old does a child have to be before allowed to speak to the judge about who is preferred as primary custodial parent?

It depends upon the judge. There is no set age at which children are allowed to speak to the judge about their preferences as to custody.

If either you or your spouse want to have the judge listen to what your child has to say, a request is ordinarily made to the judge to have the child speak to the judge in the judge's office (chambers) rather than from the witness stand. The judge might decide to allow the attorneys for each party to be present with the child.

Although it is unlikely, it is possible that the judge may also allow the attorneys to question the child. If you have concerns about the other parent learning what your child says to the judge, talk to your lawyer.

Typically, the testimony of the child is made "on the record," that is, in the presence of a court reporter. This is so that the testimony can be transcribed later in the event of an appeal.

In addition to the age of a child, a judge may consider such facts as the child's maturity and personality in determining whether an interview in chambers, of the child by the judge, will be helpful to the custody decision-making process.

Remember, once a child has reached the age of fourteen in Georgia, the child will have the right to select which parent he or she wants to live with. Oftentimes this selection is accomplished by the child signing an affidavit stating his or her selection. This is known as an *election*. It is presumed that living with the selective parent is in the child's best interest. However, the court is not obligated to follow this child's wishes and the court can instead determine that it is not in the child's best interest to live with the selected parent.

If your child is between the ages of eleven and fourteen, then the judge will consider your child's selection, but the judge shall have complete discretion in making the determination of what is in your child's best interest, and the child's desires shall not be controlling.

Judges usually talk to children younger than age eleven only when there are special circumstances that have to be considered.

8.18   Will my attorney want to speak with my children?

In most cases your attorney won't ask to speak with your children. An exception might be where custody is disputed or where either parent has made allegations of abuse or neglect.

Not all attorneys are trained in appropriate interviewing techniques for children, especially for younger children. If the attorney has not spent a lot of time with children or is not familiar with child development, the interview may not provide meaningful information. Don't hesitate to ask your attorney about his or her prior experience in working with children before you agree to an interview of your child.

If your attorney asks to meet with your child, provide some background information about your child first. Let your attorney know your child's personality, interests, and any topics that might upset your child. This background will help the attorney exercise the care essential any time a professional questions a child.

If you are concerned that going to your attorney's office for an interview will cause undue anxiety for your child, ask your attorney whether the interview can take place in a setting that would be more comfortable for your child. This might be a public place or your home.

8.19   What is a guardian *ad litem*? Why is one appointed?

In custody cases, a guardian *ad litem* is an individual who is appointed by the court to represent the best interest of the child. The guardian *ad litem* (sometimes referred to as the *GAL*), typically an attorney, is directed by the judge to conduct an investigation on the issue of custody. An easy way to understand a GAL is to picture the person as a social worker who is appointed to look out for your child's best interest.

The guardian *ad litem* may be called as a witness by you or the other parent to give testimony of the knowledge gained by the investigation. For example, testimony might address observed unsafe housing conditions of a parent. In some cases the attorneys may agree that a written report prepared by the guardian *ad litem* be received into evidence for the judge's consideration.

8.20 How might a videotape or DVD of my child help my custody case?

It all depends on the context, but generally videotapes are not a good idea. It would be better to present pictures to the judge. One thing to be concerned with regarding video is the presumption that it is intruding on the child's life. People act different when they are being filmed, and this can interject your child into your custody dispute, which the judge will not like. Also be careful not to go overboard and get illegal video of the other parent interacting with the child. Any video recording should be addressed with your attorney beforehand so that your attorney can inform you of the judge's position on this conduct.

Talk to your attorney about whether a videotape would be helpful in your case. If your attorney recommends making a videotape, talk about what scenes to include, the length of the video, keeping the original tapes, and the editing process.

A videotape of your child's day-to-day life may help the judge learn more about your child's needs. The video should show routines in your child's day, including challenging moments such as bedtime or disciplining. It can demonstrate how your child interacts with you, siblings, and other important people in your family's life. The judge can see your child's room, home, and neighborhood.

8.21 Why might I not be awarded custody?

You will not be awarded custody if the judge determines that you are not fit to be a custodial parent. You may also not be awarded custody in the event the judge determines that, although you are fit to be awarded custody, it is in your child's best interest that custody is awarded to the other parent.

Determinations of your fitness to be a custodial parent and of the best interest of your child will largely depend upon the facts of your case. Reasons why a parent might be found to be unfit include a history of physical abuse, alcohol or drug abuse, or mental health problems that affect the ability to parent. A judge's ruling on the best interest of a child is based upon numerous factors.

A decision by the judge that the other parent should have custody does not require a conclusion that you are an unfit parent. Even if the judge determines that both you and the other parent are fit to have custody, the judge may nevertheless decide that it is in the best interest of your child that only one of you be awarded custody.

8.22 Does joint physical custody always mean equal time at each parent's house?

Joint physical custody does not necessarily mean an equal division of parenting time, nor does it require that the child flip-flop every other week between two homes, but in order to be joint physical custody then there has to be something close to 50/50 time.

Whether it is sole or joint custody, you and the other parent can agree to share parenting time in a way that best serves your children. An example would be where you and your spouse agree to joint legal custody, but you will have physical custody with your child residing primarily with you.

It can also be helpful to remember that day-to-day decisions, such as a child's daily routine, will usually be made by the parent who has the child that day.

8.23 What are some of the risks of joint custody?

Joint custody may be a good idea when both parents willingly consent to it and when the parties have been separated for a period of time so their ability and willingness to decide matters focuses on the child's needs, not their own. Joint custody can work when the parents have demonstrated an ability to reach decisions regarding their children without the involvement of attorneys or the court.

Joint custody requires healthy communication between you and the other parent. Without it, you are at risk for conflict, stress, and delay when making important decisions for your child. If communication with the other parent regarding your child is poor, think carefully before agreeing to joint custody.

If you share joint legal custody and are unable to reach agreement on a major decision, such as a child's school or child-care provider, you and your former spouse may be required to return to mediation or to court to resolve your dispute. This can lead to delays in decision making for matters important to your child, increased conflict, and further legal fees.

If joint legal custody is agreed to, then the judge will require you to elect a tie-breaker for major decisions if there is a disagreement. Review the Sample Parenting Plan in the Appendix for more details regarding tie-breakers.

8.24 If my spouse is awarded physical custody of my child, how much time will our child spend with me?

Parenting time schedules for noncustodial parents vary from case to case. As in the determination of custody, the best interest of the child is what a court considers in determining the parenting time schedule. Among the factors that can impact a parenting time schedule are the past history of parenting time, the age and needs of the child, and the parents' work schedules.

If you and the other parent are willing to reach your own agreement about the parenting time schedule, you are likely to be more satisfied with it than with one imposed by a judge. Because the two of you know your child's needs, your family traditions, and your personal preferences, you can design a plan uniquely suited to your child's best interest.

If you and the other parent are unable to reach an agreement on a parenting time schedule, either on your own or with the assistance of your lawyers or a mediator, the judge will decide the schedule.

8.25 What is a *parenting plan*?

A *parenting plan* is a document that details how you and the other parent will be parenting your child after the divorce. Among the issues addressed in a parenting plan are:

- Custody, both legal and physical
- Parenting time, including specific times for:
    * Regular school year
    * Holidays
    * Birthdays
    * Mother's Day and Father's Day
    * Summer
    * School breaks
- Phone access to the child
- Communication regarding the child

- Access to records regarding the child
- Notice regarding parenting time
- Attendance at the child's activities
- Decision making regarding the child
- Exchange of information such as addresses, phone numbers, and care providers

Detailed parenting plans are good for children as well as for parents. They increase clarity for the parents, provide security for the child in knowing what to expect, reduce conflict, and lower the risk of needing to return to court for a modification of your divorce decree.

See the Appendix for a Sample Parenting Plan.

8.26   What is *standard visitation*?

Standard visitation is what many attorneys and judges refer to when discussing parenting time. It is the "default" schedule that many courts adhere to when the parents cannot reach agreement upon a schedule.

Standard visitation refers to alternating weekends and (sometimes) one evening during the week for the noncustodial parent. Additionally, it calls for holidays with the children to be alternated and for Mother's Day and Father's Day to be spent with the appropriate parent. Holiday parenting time supersedes the regular weekly schedule for parenting time.

Talk with your attorney about whether a standard visitation arrangement is best for your child. In may be that the circumstances of your family call for a different arrangement that better meets your child's needs.

8.27   I don't think it's safe for my children to have any contact with my spouse. How can I prove this to the judge?

Talk with your attorney about a plan for the protection of you and your children. Options might include a protection order, supervised visitation, or certain restrictions on the other parent's parenting time.

Make sure you have an attorney who understands your concerns for the welfare of your children. If your attorney is not taking your worry about the safety of your children seriously, you may be better served by an attorney with a greater understanding of the issues in your case.

Give your attorney a complete history of the facts upon which you base your belief that your children are not safe with the other parent. Although the most recent facts are often the most relevant, it is important that your attorney have a clear picture of the background situation as well.

Your attorney also needs information about the other parent, such as whether the other parent is or has been:

- Using alcohol or drugs
- Treated for alcohol or drug use
- Arrested, charged, or convicted of crimes of violence
- In possession of firearms
- Subject to a protection order for harassment or violence

8.28 My spouse keeps threatening to get custody because there were no witnesses to the abuse and I can't prove it. Is that right?

No. Most domestic violence is not witnessed by others, and judges know this.

If you have been a victim of abusive behavior by the other parent, or if you have witnessed your children as victims, your testimony is likely to be the most compelling evidence.

Be sure to tell your attorney about anyone who may have either seen the other parent's behavior or spoken to you or your children right after an abusive incident. They may be important witnesses in your custody case.

8.29 I am concerned about protecting my child from abuse by my spouse. Which types of past abuse by my spouse are important to tell my attorney?

Keeping your child safe is your top priority. So that your attorney can help you protect your child, give him or her a full history of the following behavior by your spouse:

- Hitting, kicking, pushing, shoving, or slapping you or your child
- Sexual abuse
- Threats to harm you or the child

113

- Threats to abduct your child
- Destruction of property
- Torture or other harm to pets
- Requiring your child to keep secrets

The process of writing down past events may help you to remember other incidents of abuse that you had forgotten. Be as complete as possible.

8.30 What documents or objects should I give my attorney to help prove the history of domestic violence by my spouse?

The following may be useful exhibits if your case goes to court:

- Photographs of injuries
- Photographs of damaged property
- Abusive or threatening notes, letters, or e-mails
- Abusive or threatening voice messages
- Your journal entries about abuse
- Police reports
- Medical records
- Court records
- Criminal and traffic records
- Damaged property, such as torn clothing

Discuss with your attorney any of these that you are able to obtain and ask your attorney whether others can be acquired through a subpoena or other means.

8.31 How can I get the other parent's visitation to be supervised?

If you are concerned about the safety of your children when they are with the other parent, talk to your attorney. It may be that a protection order is warranted to terminate or limit the other parent's contact with your children. Alternatively, it is possible to ask the judge to consider certain court orders intended to better protect your children.

Ask your attorney whether, under the facts of your case, the judge would consider any of the following court orders:

- Supervised visits
- Exchanges of the children in a public place
- Parenting class for the other parent
- Anger management or other rehabilitative program for the other parent
- A prohibition against drinking by the other parent when with the children

Judges have differing approaches to cases where children are at risk. Recognize that there are also often practical considerations, such as cost or the availability of people to supervise visits. Urge your attorney to advocate zealously for court orders to protect your children from harm by the other parent.

8.32 I want to talk to my spouse about our child, but all I get is a lot of argument. How can I communicate without it always turning into a fight?

Because conflict is high between you and the other parent, consider the following:

- Ask your attorney to help you obtain a court order for custody and parenting time that is specific and detailed. This lowers the amount of necessary communication between you and the other parent.

- Put as much information in writing as possible. Consider using e-mail, mail, or fax, especially for less urgent communication.

- Avoid criticisms of the other parent's parenting.

- Avoid instructing the other parent regarding how to parent.

- Be factual, concise, and businesslike.

- Acknowledge to the other parent the good parental qualities he or she displays, such as being concerned, attentive, or generous.

- Keep your child out of any conflicts.

By focusing on your own behavior, conflict with the other parent has the potential to decrease.

8.33 Should I call the police if our child is not returned from parenting time at the agreed-upon time?

Calling the police should be done only as a last resort and if you feel that your child is at risk for abuse or neglect, or if you have been advised by your attorney that such a call is warranted. The involvement of law enforcement officials in parental conflict can result in far greater trauma to a child than a late return at the end of a parenting time.

The appropriate response to a child not being returned according to a court order depends upon the circumstances. If the problem is a recurring one, talk to your attorney regarding your options. It may be that a change in the schedule would be in the best interest of your child.

Regardless of the behavior of the other parent, make every effort to keep your child out of any conflicts between the parents.

8.34 If I have full custody, may I move out of state without the permission of the court?

Yes, but you will be required to provide the other parent with notice prior to moving. A custodial parent in Georgia is not required to obtain permission of the court prior to moving out of state with a child. Georgia requires that any parent changing residences must provide the other parent with at least thirty days' prior notice of the anticipated change and must also include the full address of the new residence.

If your former spouse objects to your move, they must apply to the court for an order for a change of custody or a modification (but your spouse will have to show how this would negatively affect the child) and have a court hearing for the judge to decide what is in the child's best interest.

You may have to prove that you have a legitimate reason for the move, such as a better job or a transfer of your new spouse's employment. You may also have to prove that the move is in the best interest of your child.

8.35 What factors does the court consider when determining the best interest of the child when relocation is the issue?

In determining your child's best interest, the court may consider many factors. These factors can be the same as the factors the court uses when determining the child's best interest for a custody action. These can include your child's ties to Georgia, the quality of the community you want to move to, your reason for the move, your child's relationship with other relatives, and your child's relationship with the other parent. If you're considering an out-of-state move, talk to your attorney immediately. Do so even if you have not finalized your plans. There are important facts for you to gather as soon as possible about potential housing, school, and day care.

8.36 After the divorce, can my spouse legally take our children out of the state during parenting time? Out of the country?

It depends upon the terms of the court order as set forth in your decree.

If you are concerned about your children being out of Georgia with the other parent, discuss the possibility of some of these decree provisions regarding out-of-state travel with your child:

- Limits on the duration or distance for out-of-state travel with the child
- Notice requirements
- Information on phone numbers
- Information on physical addresses
- E-mail address contact information
- Possession of the child's passport with the court
- Posting of bond by the other parent prior to travel
- Requiring a court order for travel outside the country

Although judges are not ordinarily concerned about short trips across state lines, you should let your attorney know if you are concerned that your child may be abducted by the other parent so that reasonable safeguards may be put in place.

One way to safeguard against international trips is to require a provision that clearly gives you authority over the child's passport.

8.37 If I am not given physical custody, what rights do I have regarding medical records and medical treatment for my child?

Regardless of which parent has physical custody, state law generally allows both parents to have access to the medical records of their children and to make emergency medical decisions.

8.38 If I'm not the primary caregiver, how will I know what's going on at my child's school? What rights to records do I have there?

Regardless of your custodial status, you have a right to access to your child's school records.

Develop a relationship with your child's teachers and the school staff. Request to be put on the school's mailing list for all notices. Find out what is necessary for you to get copies of important school information and report cards.

Communicate with the other parent to both share and receive information about your child's progress in school. This will enable you to support your child and each other through any challenging periods of your child's education. It also enables you to share a mutual pride in your child's successes.

Regardless of which parent has custody, your child will benefit from both parents' involvement by the parents' participation in parent-teacher conferences, attendance at school events, help with school homework, and positive communication between the parents.

8.39 What if my child does not want to go for the parenting time? Can my former spouse force the child to go?

If your child is resisting going with the other parent, it can first be helpful to determine the underlying reason. Consider these questions:

- What is your child's stated reason for not wanting to go?
- Does your child appear afraid, anxious, or sad?

- Do you have any concerns regarding your child's safety while with the other parent?

- Have you prepared your child for being with the other parent, speaking about the experience with enthusiasm and encouragement?

- Is it possible your child is perceiving your anxiety about the situation and is consequently having the same reaction?

- Have you provided support for your child's transition to the other home, such as completing fun activities in your home well in advance of the other parent's starting time for parenting?

- Have you spoken to the other parent about your child's behavior?

- Can you provide anything that will make your child's time with the other parent more comfortable, such as a favorite toy or blanket?

- Have you established clear routines that support your child to be ready to go with the other parent with ease, such as packing a backpack or saying good-bye to a family pet?

The reason for a child's reluctance to go with the other parent may be as simple as being sad about leaving you or as serious as being a victim of abuse in the other parent's home. It is important to look at this situation closely to determine the best response.

Judges treat compliance with court orders for parenting time seriously. If one parent believes that the other is intentionally interfering with parenting time or the parent-child relationship, it can result in further litigation. At the same time, you want to know that your child is safe. Talk with your attorney about the best approach in your situation.

8.40 What steps can I take to prevent my spouse from getting the children in the event of my death?

Unless the other parent is not fit to have custody, the surviving parent has the legal right to custody of the child in the event of your death.

All parents should have a will naming a guardian for their children. In the event you do not intend to name the other parent, talk with your attorney. Seek counsel about how to best document and preserve the evidence that will be needed to prove that the other parent is unfit to have custody in the event of your death.

9

Child Support

*Both parents have the legal and moral duty to provide
love, nurturing, and support—emotional, physical, and
financial. Your duty began at conception, carries through
a divorce, and will likely continue until you are enjoying
grandchildren and beyond.*
Accept it. Embrace it. Enjoy it.

Whether you will be paying child support or receiving it, it is often the subject of much concern. Will I receive enough support to take care of my children? Will I have enough money to live on after I pay my child support? How will I make ends meet?

Most parents want to provide for their children. Today, the child-support laws make it possible for parents to have a better understanding of their obligation to support their children. The mechanisms for both payment and receipt of child support are now more clearly defined, and help is available for collecting support if it's not paid.

The Georgia Child Support Guidelines, the Child Support Payment Center, and the Child Support Enforcement office all help to simplify the child-support system. As you learn more about them, matters regarding child support that appear complex in the beginning can eventually become routine for you and the other parent.

9.1   What determines whether I will get child support?

Whether you will receive child support depends upon a number of factors. These may include how much time your child is living in your household, which parent has primary physical custody, and each parent's ability to pay support.

If your current spouse is not the biological or adoptive parent of your child, you will more than likely not receive child support from your spouse. You should discuss these specifics with your lawyer.

If you have physical custody of your child, it is likely your current spouse will be ordered to pay support for any children born or adopted during the marriage to your current spouse.

9.2   Can I request child support even if I do not meet the six-month residency requirement for a divorce in Georgia?

Yes. Even though you may not have met the requirements to obtain a divorce, you have a right to seek support for your children. Talk to your attorney about pursuing a private action for child support. If you cannot afford to hire an attorney, then you can visit the Georgia Department of Human Services website at http://dcss.dhs.georgia.gov/ for information about how to apply in your Georgia county of residence at the Office of Child Support. You may apply for help to get child support from the other parent. However, it is important to remember that the Georgia court must have valid jurisdiction over the parent. To have valid jurisdiction requires the other parent to be a *bona fide* resident of the state and be properly served with a copy of the court filing and subpoena. If Georgia does not have valid jurisdiction over the other parent, the Child Support Enforcement office can initiate an action to be forwarded to the other parent's home county in Georgia or another state.

9.3   Can I get temporary support while waiting for custody to be decided?

A judge has authority to enter a temporary order for custody and child support. This order usually remains in place until a final decree establishing custody is entered. In most cases a hearing for temporary custody and support can be held shortly after the filing of the complaint for divorce.

9.4 What is *temporary support* and how soon can I get it?

Temporary support is paid for the support of a spouse or a child. It is paid sometime after the divorce petition is filed and continues until your final decree of divorce is entered by the court or until your case is dismissed.

If you are in need of temporary support, talk to your attorney at your first opportunity. If you and the other parent are unable to agree upon the amount of temporary support to be paid each month, talk to your attorney. If an agreement is not reached, it is likely that your attorney will file a motion for temporary support, asking the judge to decide how much the support should be and when it will start.

Because there are a number of steps to getting a temporary child-support order, don't delay in discussing your need for support with your attorney. Child support generally will not be ordered for any period prior to the filing of a request for it with the court.

The following are the common steps in the process:

- You discuss your need for a temporary child-support order with your attorney.

- Your attorney requests a hearing date from the judge and prepares the necessary documents.

- A temporary hearing is held.

- The temporary order is signed by the judge.

- The other parent's employer is notified to begin withholding your support from the other parent's paychecks.

- The other parent's employer sends the support to the Georgia Support Enforcement office.

- Georgia's Child Support Enforcement office sends the money to you.

If the other parent is not paying you support voluntarily, time is of the essence in obtaining a temporary order for support. This should be one of the first issues you discuss with your attorney.

9.5 How soon does my spouse have to start paying support for the children?

Your spouse may begin paying you support voluntarily at any time. A temporary order for support will give you the right to collect the support if your spouse stops paying. Talk to your attorney about court hearings for temporary support in your county. You may have to wait for a week or longer before your temporary hearing can be held. It is possible that the judge will not order child support to start until the first of the following month. Georgia law requires each parent to provide support for his or her children so it is important to discuss the timing of support with your attorney.

9.6 How is the amount of child support I will receive or I must pay computed?

The Georgia Child Support Guidelines were created by the Georgia legislature to set forth the standards by which your child support is calculated. According to the guidelines, both parents have a duty to contribute to the support of their children in proportion to their respective net incomes. As a result, both your gross income (pretax) and the gross income of the other parent will factor into the child-support calculation.

Other factors the court may consider include:

- The additional cost of health insurance for the child
- Child-care expenses
- Education expenses
- Other children you are legally responsible for
- Regularly paid support for other children
- Substantial fluctuations of annual earnings by either parent
- The amount of contributions to certain retirement plans
- Which parent claims the children as exemptions for tax purposes

Child support that is higher or lower than what the guidelines provide for may be awarded in certain cases, for example:

- When either parent or child has extraordinary medical costs

- When the child is enrolled in day care or other child care is needed
- When a child is disabled with special needs
- For juveniles placed in foster care
- When the parents live far apart (referred to as a travel deviation)
- Whenever the application of the guidelines in an individual case would be unjust or inappropriate

When a judge orders an amount of support that is different from the guideline amount, it is referred to as a *deviation*. Due to the complexity of calculations under the guidelines, many attorneys use computer software to calculate child support.

9.7 Will the type of custody arrangement or the amount of parenting time I have impact the amount of child support I receive?

It can. Sharing physical custody can dramatically lower child-support amounts. For this reason, it is essential that you discuss child support with your attorney prior to reaching any agreements with the other parent regarding custody or parenting time.

If you intend to mediate custody or parenting time, be sure to talk with your attorney in advance regarding how these decisions can affect your child support.

However, you should be aware that Georgia courts consider visitation and child support as separate and one is not tied to the other.

9.8 Is overtime pay considered in the calculation of child support?

Generally, yes, if your overtime is a regular part of your employment and you can actually expect to earn it regularly. The judge can consider your work history, the degree of control you have over your overtime, and the nature of the field in which you work.

9.9 Will rental income be factored into my child support, or just my salary?

Generally, yes. Georgia child support is based on a parent's gross income from all sources. Therefore, if you are receiving an additional $200 per month from your rental property, then your gross monthly income will be increased by this $200.

9.10 My spouse has a college degree, but refuses to get a job. Will the court consider this in determining the amount of child support?

The *earning capacity* of the other parent may be considered instead of current income. The court can look at the other parent's work history, education, skills, health, and job opportunities.

If you believe the other parent is earning substantially less than he or she is capable of earning (underemployed or underreporting), provide your attorney with details. Ask about making a case for child support based on earning capacity instead of actual income. Georgia refers to this an *imputed income.*

9.11 Will I get the child support directly from my spouse or from the state?

It depends. Georgia does not require child support to be withheld from the payor's employer, unless there is good cause shown for why it should be. Most of the time the payor will pay the other parent directly. However, more and more parties are seeking to have their employers withhold child support from employee wages just as they withhold taxes or retirement because it takes away substantial stress on both sides and leaves less room for conflict.

If the payor parent is not paying the other parent directly, then it's possible to have the child-support amount withheld by the payor's employer. The payor's employer then submits the child-support payments, usually electronically, to the *Georgia Family Support Registry (FSR),* now at a centralized office in Atlanta. The FSR's Payment Center then transmits electronically the child support to the bank account of the parent receiving support.

9.12 If my spouse sends in a child-support payment to the state, how quickly will the state mail me a check?

A number of factors affect how quickly your child-support payment will be paid to you after it is received by the Payment Center, such as whether it is an out-of-state check or a certified check.

The Payment Center can mail you a check for your child-support or you may decide to receive it by direct deposit. It may take three to five business days for processing through the mail. More information can be found on the Georgia Family Support Registry (FSR) website at http://dcss.dhs.georgia.gov/family-support-registry.

9.13 Is there any reason not to pay or receive payments directly to or from my spouse once the court has entered a child-support order?

It depends. Direct payments of child support between the parents can result in misunderstandings. The payor may have intended the money to pay a child-support payment, but the parent receiving the support may have thought it was extra money to help with the child's expenses.

If a direct payment is made to the other parent, avoid cash payments—unless you are prepared to obtain and preserve a receipt signed by the other parent for every payment. It is usually wiser to use a money order or a personal check for each payment so you may prove payments were made. This is important so that your records remain accurate. If no receipt is kept for a direct payment, it may later be considered a gift, not a child-support payment. If you do not care enough to keep track, the judge may not care enough to sort it out.

The payment of support through the Georgia Family Support Registry (FSR) protects both parents. If the payment is made through the (FSR), the state's records will show a record of payment and indicate if child-support payments are current or in arrears.

The concerns with using the FSR are the delay in receiving payment and the cost (approximately $2 per month) for using the service.

9.14 Can I go to the courthouse to pick up my child-support payment?

No. In the past, payments for child support were made to the clerk of the court in the county where the child-support order was entered. Today, all child-support payments in Georgia are processed through a central location (Atlanta) at the Georgia Family Support Registry (FSR).

9.15 How soon can I expect my child-support payments to start arriving?

A number of factors may affect the date on which you will begin receiving your child support. Here are the usual steps in the process if the payments are being withheld by the employer and paid to the Georgia Family Support Registry:

- A child-support amount and start date for the support are decided either by agreement between you and your spouse or by the judge.

- Either your attorney or your spouse's attorney prepares the court order.

- The attorney who did not write the court order reviews and approves it.

- The court order is taken to the judge for signature.

- Your spouse signs a Notice to Withhold Income form and delivers it to the employer, asking that child support be withheld from future paychecks.

- Your spouse's employer withholds the support from the paycheck.

- The child support is transferred by the employer into the Georgia Family Support Registry (FSR).

- The Payment Center sends the money to you, either by direct deposit or mail.

As you can see, there are a lot of steps in this process. Plan your budget knowing that the initial payment of child support will take longer than you might like.

9.16 Will some amount of child support be withheld from every paycheck?

It depends upon the employer's policy and how you are paid. If support is due on the first of the month, the employer has the full month to withhold the amount ordered to be paid. If an employer issues paychecks twice a month, it is possible that half of the support will be withheld from each check and paid to the Georgia Family Support Registry (FSR) at the end of the month.

If an employer issues checks every other week, which is twenty-six pay periods per year, there will be some months in which a third paycheck is issued. Consequently, it is possible that no child support will be withheld from the wages paid in that third check of the month or that some checks will be for less than 50 percent of the monthly amount due.

Example: Suppose child support is $650 per month and the employee/payor is paid every other Friday, or twenty-six times per year. The yearly support is $7,800 ($650/month times twelve months). The employer may withhold $300 per biweekly paycheck for child support ($7,800 divided into twenty-six paydays). Although for most months the support received will be two payment of $300 each, some months will have a third paycheck, for a total of $900 that month. However, averaged over the year, the amount will be $650 per month using this example.

Over time, child-support payments typically fall into a routine schedule, which makes it easier for both the payor and the recipient of support to plan their budgets.

9.17 If my spouse has income other than from an employer (such as from self-employment), is it still possible to get a court order to withhold my child support from that income?

Yes. Child support can be automatically withheld from most sources of income. These may include self-employment, unemployment, worker's compensation, retirement plans, and investment income.

9.18 The spouse I am divorcing is not the biological parent of my child. Can I still collect child support from my current spouse?

Possibly, but not likely. Although your spouse may be ordered to pay child support under certain circumstances, it is rare. Among the factors the court will consider is whether your spouse has fully assumed the role of a parent to your child, whether the child has formed a parental bond as if a virtual adoption has occurred, and whether you have been relying on those actions. However, if the child's biological parent is active in the child's life, then the answer will usually be no.

Discuss the facts of your case with your attorney in detail. When you are clear about what will be in the best interest of your child, your attorney can support you in developing a strategy for your case that takes into consideration not only child support but also the future relationship of your spouse with your child.

However, this is the rare case, and in most circumstances your spouse will not be responsible for child support for a child who is not their biological child when no legal formal adoption has taken place.

9.19 Can I collect child support from both the biological parent and the adoptive parent of my child?

You cannot collect support from both. When your child was adopted, the biological parent's duty to support your child ended and the adoptive parent's duty began. However, it may be possible for you to collect past-due child support from the period of time before the adoption.

9.20 What happens with child support when our children go to the other parent's home for summer vacation? Is child support still due and payable?

The general answer is that child support is still payable in full even during summer vacation visitation. However, this answer also depends upon the settlement agreement of the parties, if any, or the court order in your case, and the terms under which a deviation is allowed from the norm for child support.

Georgia does not recognize *abatement* (temporary stoppage or reduction during visitation) of child support as some states do.

Before your divorce decree is entered by the court, talk with your attorney about child-support deviations regarding parenting time and the potential consequences if you are anticipating that the parent paying support will have the child for an extended period and how some reduction might be implemented if both parents consent.

9.21 After the divorce, if I choose to live with my new partner rather than marry, can I still collect child support?

Yes. Although spousal support (alimony) may end if you live with your partner, child support does not terminate for this reason.

9.22 Can I still collect child support if I move to another state?

Yes. A move out of state will not end your right to receive child support. However, the amount of child support could be changed if other circumstances change, such as income or costs for exercising parenting time. A new order will be required before any change in amount is required.

9.23 Can I expect to continue to receive child support if I remarry?

Yes. Your child support will continue even if you remarry.

9.24 How long can I expect to receive child support?

Under Georgia law, child support is ordinarily ordered to be paid until the child dies, marries, is emancipated (becomes self-supporting), or reaches the age of eighteen. Georgia also commonly accepts the parties' agreements that child support will continue after age eighteen until the child graduates high school—but not after the child attains the age of twenty.

9.25   Does interest accrue on past-due child support?

Yes, interest accrues on past-due child support. The interest rate should be set forth in your decree based upon the interest rate in effect under state law on the date your decree is entered.

9.26   What can I do if my former spouse refuses to pay child support?

If your former spouse is not paying child support, you may take action to enforce the court order either with the help of your attorney or with the assistance of your local Child-Support Enforcement office. Visit the Georgia Family Support Registry (FSR) website at http://dcss.dhs.georgia.gov/family-support-registry for a listing of the offices and addresses of child-support services that may help you.

In most counties, the elected county prosecuting attorney (the district attorney) is responsible for enforcement of child support.

You can also pursue a contempt action arguing that the party is violating the order of the court by not paying. If your former spouse is found in contempt of court for the intentional failure to pay support, the judge could impose jail for contempt or order other relief.

The judge may order payment of both the current amount of support and an additional amount to be paid each month until the past-due child support (referred to as *arrearages*) is paid in full. You may request that your former spouse's state and federal tax refunds be sent directly to the Georgia Family Support Registry (FSR). It may also be possible to garnish a checking or savings account.

A payor parent's driver's license may also be suspended if that parent falls behind in child-support payments. If sufficient evidence is presented to the court that the accumulated support arrearage is equivalent to or greater than the current support due for sixty days, the court may order the Georgia Department of Driver Services to suspend the payor parent's driver's license or deny an application for a driver's license.

However, if there is a payment plan for the payment of arrearages, then the license will not be suspended.

To review, if you are not receiving child support, you have three options:

- Call your attorney.
- Call Child Support Enforcement in Georgia (the number is (844) 694-2347.
- Contact the Georgia Department of Human Services, Division of Child Support Services website (http://dcss.dhs.georgia.gov/).

9.27 At what point will the state help me collect back child support, and what methods do they use?

It depends. Call Child Support Enforcement in Georgia at (844) 694-2347 and select 1 for Division of Child Support Services, or visit the Georgia Department of Human Services, Division of Child Support Services website at http://dcss.dhs.georgia.gov/.

9.28 I live outside Georgia. Will the money I spend on airline tickets to visit my children impact my child support?

It might. If you expect to spend large sums of money for transportation in order to have visitation or parenting time with your children, talk to your attorney about how this might be taken into consideration when determining the amount of child support. Georgia child-support worksheets have the option to include a *deviation* for visitation-related travel expenses. These deviations are discretionary by the judge. It is important to discuss these anticipated expenses with your lawyer prior to agreement as to the amount of child support to be paid.

9.29 After the divorce, can my former spouse, instead of paying me, substitute buying sprees with the child for child-support payments?

No. Purchases of gifts and clothing for a child do not relieve your former spouse from an obligation to pay you the mandated child support.

9.30 Are expenses such as child care supposed to be taken out of my child support?

It depends on the wording of the order for child support. Georgia's child-support worksheets allow for the inclusion of calculations for expenses for child care. Therefore, the most thorough method of computing child support would be to add the additional expenses for child care on the work sheets. The guidelines provide that each parent pay a percentage of the school-related day-care expenses in addition to the "presumptive amount of child support." If this is the case, then the other parent will pay you a certain amount of child support and you would be required to pay for child care and other expenses out of the total amount (because, in theory, the amount is greater if there is child care versus no child care).

Other expenses for your child, such as clothing, school lunches, and the cost for activities, are ordinarily paid for by you if you are receiving child support according to the guidelines, unless the court order in your case provides otherwise.

9.31 Can my spouse be required by the decree to pay for our child's private elementary and high school education?

It depends. Oftentimes this will depend on what is in your child's best interest. The Georgia child-support worksheets do allow for a calculation of additional educational expenses (for things like private schools). The child-support worksheets refer to these costs as *extraordinary educational expenses.*

If you want the other parent to share this expense for your child, talk it over with your attorney. Be sure to provide your attorney with information regarding tuition, fees, and other expenses related to private education and explain why public school would not be in the child's best interest.

9.32 Can my spouse be required by the decree to contribute financially to our child's college education?

In Georgia, the legal duty of a parent to support a child does not include payment for college education. However, if the other parent agrees to pay this expense, it can be included in the final decree and it will be an enforceable court order. Such a provision is ordinarily included in a divorce decree only as a result of a negotiated consent settlement.

If your decree includes a provision for payment of college education expenses, be sure it is specific. Terms to consider include:

- What expenses are included? For example, tuition, room and board, books, fees, travel, and other anticipated expenses.
- Is there a limit? For example, "up to the level of the cost of attendance at Georgia Southern University" or a certain dollar amount as may be agreed.
- When is payment due?
- For what period of time? For how many years is the obligation to continue?
- Does the obligation end if less than a certain grade point average is earned or if the child is no longer in good standing as a full-time student? Often, once eligibility ends, the obligation to pay is forever ended.
- Are there any limits on the type of education or major that will be paid for?

The greater the clarity in such a provision, the lower the risk for misunderstanding or conflict years later.

10

Alimony

One spouse may truly feel:
I am not paying one penny in alimony.
My spouse made my life hell and ruined me financially (or
was unfaithful). My spouse deserves nothing.
The other spouse may truly feel:
I want to inflict punishment. I did everything possible to
provide a happy home for my spouse. I was abused, and now I
want to inflict financial pain. I want all I can get.

The mere mention of the word *alimony* might stir your emotions and start your stomach churning. If your spouse filed for divorce and sought alimony, you might see it as a double injustice—your marriage is ending and salt in the wound is you must now finance the divorce, whether you want it or not.

If you are seeking spousal support, you might feel hurt and confused that your spouse is resistant to helping to support you, even though you interrupted your career to be a stay-at-home parent to care for the children and be the homemaker.

Learning more about Georgia's laws on *alimony,* also referred to as *spousal support,* can help you move from your emotional reaction to it to the reality of possible outcomes in your case. Uncertainty about the precise amount of alimony that may be awarded or the number of years it might be paid is not unusual. Work closely with your attorney. Analyze the needs of both you and your spouse balanced against income, expenses, and ability to pay. Be realistic.

With the help of your attorney, you will get an idea of the other spouse's real *ability* to pay and your own real *need* for financial support. When two people become a family to share household expenses, their combined budget is likely 75 percent of what they were separately spending. The greater disposable combined income likely raised the standard of living for the couple.

Upon separation and divorce, the combined living-apart budgets for both can rise to double or triple the previous family combined budget. Simply stated, belt tightening is usually required by both parties after divorce.

Your lawyer will help you plan the best course of action to take toward an alimony decision, one you can live with after your divorce is over. Just remember, each case is different and Georgia law does not provide a set formula for alimony. So, the facts and circumstances in your particular case, decided by the judge or jury, will determine alimony in the court's sound discretion.

10.1 Which gets calculated first, child support or alimony?

Generally, child support is calculated first because child support is calculated based on gross income (pretax). Spousal support is determined from the income that is available to be paid after child support. Many factors are taken into account when determining an appropriate amount of alimony, if any.

10.2 What's the difference between *spousal support* and *alimony*?

In Georgia, *alimony* and *spousal support* have the same meaning.

10.3 Are their different types of alimony?

In Georgia, there are different classifications of alimony. The two most common types of alimony that can be awarded are: *lump-sum alimony* and *periodic alimony*. The court may award alimony for either a fixed period of time to enable you or your spouse to obtain further training or education to be more fully self-supporting—this is often referred to as *rehabilitative alimony* or *transitional alimony*. Alternatively, the court may determine that, based on the facts of your case, you or your spouse are entitled to *permanent alimony*. Generally, permanent alimony is reserved for those cases where there is a lengthy marriage and one spouse has the ability to provide for the other, who is in need of that support, and that dependent spouse has been so supported for the bulk of the marriage.

Alimony, in whatever form, is simply a support of one spouse supplied by the other spouse. In its strictest sense, alimony is constituted by payments of money made at regular intervals.

10.4   How will I know if I am eligible to receive alimony?

Talk with your attorney about whether you are a candidate for alimony.

The opinions of Georgia judges about awarding alimony vary greatly. Among the factors that may affect your eligibility to receive alimony are:

- The standard of living established during the marriage
- The length of your marriage
- Your contributions to the marriage, including the interruption of your career for the care of children or to support your spouse's career
- Your education, work history, health, income, and earning capacity
- Your overall financial situation compared to that of your spouse
- Your need for support
- The amount of time that would be necessary to train or educate either spouse so that he or she can find appropriate employment
- Your spouse's ability to pay support
- Any other factor deemed by the court as relevant, including marital misconduct of either party

Every case for alimony is unique. Providing your attorney with clear and detailed information about the facts of your marriage and current situation will increase the likelihood of a fair outcome for you.

10.5 What information should I provide to my attorney if I want alimony?

If your attorney advises that you may be a candidate for alimony, be sure to provide complete facts about your situation, including:

- A history of the interruptions in your education or career for the benefit of your spouse, including transfers or moves due to your spouse's employment
- A history of the interruptions in your education or career for raising children, including periods during which you worked part-time
- Your complete educational background, including the dates of your schooling or training and degrees earned
- Your work history, including the names of your employers, the dates of your employment, your duties, your pay, and the reason you left
- Any pensions or other benefits lost due to the interruption of your career for the benefit of the marriage
- Your health history, including any current diagnoses, treatments, limitations, and medications
- Your monthly living expenses, including anticipated future expenses such as health insurance and tax on alimony
- A complete list of debts for you and your spouse
- Income for you and your spouse, including all sources

Also include any other facts that might support your need for alimony, such as other contributions you made to the marriage, upcoming medical treatment, or a lack of jobs in the field in which you were formerly employed.

No two alimony cases are alike. The better the information your attorney has about your situation, the easier it will be to assess your case for alimony.

10.6   My spouse told me that because I had an affair during the marriage, I have no chance to get alimony even though I quit my job and have cared for our children for many years. Is it true that I have no case?

It could be. In Georgia, a party will not be entitled to alimony if it is established by a preponderance of the evidence that the separation between the parties was caused by that party's adultery or desertion. However, this is not an easy thing to prove. If you believe that this situation applies to your case, then discuss the specifics with your lawyer so that you can plan accordingly.

10.7   How is the amount of alimony calculated?

Unlike child support, there are not specific guidelines for determining the amount of alimony. A judge or jury will look at the expenses and incomes of you and your spouse, after giving consideration to the payment and receipt of any child support.

Judges and juries are given a lot of discretion to make their own decision on alimony without the benefit of specific guidelines. Consequently, the outcome of an alimony ruling by a judge or jury can be one of the most unpredictable aspects of your divorce.

Georgia commonly describes how the amount of alimony is calculated as one party's need for alimony versus the other party's ability to pay.

10.8   My spouse makes a lot more money than reported on our tax return because the income is hidden. How can I prove my spouse's real income to show what can really be afforded for alimony payments?

Alert your attorney to your concerns. Your attorney can then take a number of actions to determine your spouse's income with greater accuracy. This is likely to include:

- More thorough discovery
- An examination of check registers and bank deposits
- Reviewing purchases made in cash
- Inquiring about travel
- Depositions of third parties who have knowledge of income or spending by your spouse

- Subpoena of records of places where your spouse has made large purchases or from where income has been received
- Comparing income claimed with expenses paid

By partnering with your attorney, you may be able to build a case to establish your spouse's actual income as greater than is shown on your tax returns. If you filed joint tax returns, discuss with your attorney any other implications of erroneous information on those returns.

10.9   I want to be sure the records on the alimony I pay are accurate, especially for tax purposes. What's the best way to ensure this?

If you are paying child support in addition to spousal support, your alimony payments should be made to the Georgia Child Support Enforcement office. Alimony can be automatically withheld from your pay, just like your child support.

Even if you are not paying child support, it is still possible to have the spousal support deducted directly by your employer. This way, payment can be made directly—also known as an *income deduction order.* By avoiding direct payments to your former spouse, you both will have accurate records.

To avoid an audit, or defend an audit by the Internal Revenue Service, you must deduct the same amount of alimony that your spouse is reporting as income on your tax returns (if the type of payments you are making are taxable or deductible).

10.10 How is the purpose of alimony different from the payment of my property settlement?

Spousal support and the division of property serve two distinct purposes, even though many of the factors for determining them are the same. The purpose of alimony is to pay for your continued necessary support, whereas the purpose of a property division is to distribute the marital assets fairly between you and your spouse based on equitable principles or "fairness."

10.11   How long can alimony be expected to continue?

The modern trend in Georgia has been away from lifetime alimony awards and more toward transitional alimony. How long the alimony award will be ordered to continue, just like whether any alimony at all will be awarded, will depend upon the facts of your case and the judge's or jury's philosophy toward alimony. In general, the longer the marriage, the stronger is the case for a long-term alimony award.

An award might be made for only temporary alimony (or transitional alimony), or for a certain period of years. Talk to your attorney about the facts of your case to get a clearer picture of the possible outcomes in your situation.

10.12   Does remarriage affect an award of alimony?

It may, depending on the type of alimony that is awarded. Georgia law is very complicated when it comes to alimony. Georgia divides alimony into two main types: *lump-sum alimony* and *periodic alimony*. Georgia law is clear that all unperformed obligations for permanent alimony to a spouse shall stop upon that spouse's remarriage, unless the decree provides differently. However, if you are receiving lump-sum alimony (or a property settlement), then the payments will not stop upon the spouse's remarriage. This is true even if the lump-sum alimony is payable in installments.

If alimony is a possibility in your case then you need to address this complicated issue with your lawyer and make sure you plan for the best fit for your situation.

10.13   Can alimony be collected if I move to a different state?

Yes. The duty to pay alimony by court order does not end simply because one of you, or both or you, move to another state, unless there is a specific provision in your decree that controls that circumstance.

10.14   What can be done if alimony is not paid?

If alimony stops in violation of the court order, there are legal remedies available to enforce the court order. The judge may order the support to be taken from the payor's source of income or from a financial account. This is commonly done by an income deduction order.

If refusal to pay is intentional or willful, despite the ability to pay, an action for contempt may be initiated. In a contempt action, the payor may be ordered to appear in court and provide evidence explaining why support has not been paid. Possible consequences for contempt of court include a jail sentence and an award of attorney fees for filing the contempt action.

10.15 Can I return to court to modify alimony?

It depends. If your divorce decree provides that your alimony order is "nonmodifiable," then modification is generally not allowed. Also, if no award of alimony was made in the final decree, alimony cannot later be awarded. Georgia law is complicated in this area. Georgia distinguishes between lump-sum alimony, which is sometimes referred to as a *property settlement* and is not modifiable, and periodic alimony, which is modifiable.

It is important to discuss with your lawyer at the start of your divorce the type of alimony that is best for you. If your type of alimony is modifiable and there has been a material change in the circumstances of either you or your spouse, you may seek to have alimony modified. Examples include a serious illness or the loss of a job or the obtaining of a job.

A complaint to modify alimony for the purposes of seeking additional alimony may not be filed if the period of time for payment of periodic alimony awarded under the original decree has already expired.

If the issue of modification of alimony arises, contact your attorney at once to ensure the basis is established and evidence is preserved on the issue, with a timely motion or defense filed in the matter.

11

Division of Property

It is easier to divide property if one focuses on what he or she truly wants and needs, rather than just seek to deprive the other party of items important to the other party.

You never imagined that you would face losing the house you and your spouse so happily moved into—the house where you celebrated family traditions and spent countless hours making it "home." Your spouse wants it and the lawyers say it might even have to be sold.

During a divorce, you and your spouse will have the opportunity to agree as to who will take ownership of everything from bathroom towels to the stock portfolio.

Suddenly, you find yourself having a strong attachment to that chandelier in the dining room or the pool table in the family room. Why does the husband suddenly want the chandelier, and why would the right-handed wife want her spouse's left-handed golf clubs? Why does the collection of coins or teaspoons suddenly take on new meaning? If it is spite, or jealousy, or just pure greed, prepare to pay for litigation.

Do your best to reach agreement regarding dividing household goods. Neither the judge nor any jury will care half as much as you do about your stuff, even the important things, much less who gets the toaster or the gas grill. Choose wisely or you may be at the mercy of strangers (a jury) who *literally* could not care less. Focus on the major issues, or risk losing on important ones.

Enlist the support of your attorney in deciding which assets should be valued by an expert, such as the family business or real estate. From tax consequences to replacement value, there are many factors to consider in deciding whether to fight to keep an asset, to give it to your spouse, or to have it sold.

Like all aspects of your divorce, take one step at a time. By starting with the items most easily divided, you and your spouse can avoid paying lawyers to litigate the value of that 1980s record album collection.

It is the rare divorce where both parties get all the property they demand or think they should get from a divorce action. Therefore, it is prudent to seek the property essential to your future well-being.

11.1   What system does Georgia use for dividing property?

Georgia law provides for an equitable or fair division of the property and debts acquired during the marriage as a result of the fruits and labors of the parties during marriage. However, neither *fair division* nor *equitable division* means the division must or will be *equal division.*

Regardless of how title is held, the court can use its discretion (sound judgment) to divide the marital assets. In some cases, this may mean an equal division, but in other cases the division may not be equal, but could still be considered equitable.

The court will consider a number of factors to determine what is equitable, including your debts, the circumstances of you and your spouse, and the history of contributions to the marriage.

11.2   What does *community property* mean?

Community property is a term used in several states that have a community property system for dividing assets in a divorce. In those states, each spouse holds a one-half interest in most property acquired during the marriage. Georgia is not a community property state.

11.3   Does Georgia recognize community property?

No. Because Georgia is an equitable division state and not a community property state, community property laws do not apply in Georgia.

11.4   How is it determined who gets the house?

The first issue regarding the marital home is often a determination of who will retain possession of it while the divorce is pending. Later, it must be decided whether the house will be sold or whether it will be awarded to you or your spouse.

If you and your spouse are unable to reach agreement regarding the house, the judge (or jury) will decide who keeps it, who will pay the mortgage on the house, or whether it will be sold, and, if it is to be sold, who gets what share of the proceeds.

If you have children, then the spouse having primary physical custody might stay in the home so it is easier on the children. Being able to afford the house is also an important factor.

If staying in your house is important to you, then make sure to discuss this with your lawyer so that you can effectively plan to try to make this happen.

11.5   Should I sell the house during the divorce proceedings?

Selling your home is a big decision. To help you decide what is right for you, ask yourself these questions:

- What will be the impact on my children if the home is sold?
- Can I afford to stay in the house after the divorce?
- After the divorce, will I be willing to give the house and yard the time, money, and physical energy required for its maintenance?
- Is it necessary for me to sell the house to pay a share of the equity to my spouse, or are there other options?
- Would my life be easier if I were in a smaller or simpler home?
- Would I prefer to move closer to the support of friends and family?
- What is the state of the housing market in my community?
- What are the benefits of remaining in this home?
- Can I retain the existing mortgage or will I have to refinance?

146

Division of Property

- Will I have a higher or lower interest rate if I sell the house?
- Can I see myself living in a different home?
- Will I have the means to acquire another home?
- If I don't retain the home and my spouse asks for it, what effect will this have on my custody case?
- Will my spouse agree to the sale of the house?
- What will be the real estate commission?
- What will be the costs of preparing the house for sale?
- Is the house worth more than is owed on it or is the house "underwater" and have "negative equity" (more money is owed than what the house is valued at)?

Selling a home is more than just a legal or financial decision. Consider what is important to you in creating your life after divorce when deciding whether to sell your home.

11.6   What is meant by *equity* in my home?

Regardless of who is awarded the house, the court will consider whether the spouse not receiving the house should be compensated for the equity in the house. By *equity* we mean the difference between the value of the home and the amount owed in mortgages against the property.

For example, if the first mortgage is $150,000 and the second mortgage from a home equity loan is $10,000, the total debt owed against the house is $160,000. If your home is valued at $200,000, the equity in your home is $40,000 (the $200,000 value less the $160,000 in mortgages equals $40,000 in equity).

If one of the parties remains in the home, the issue of how to give the other party a fair share of the equity must be considered.

Unfortunately, a lot of homes have negative equity. *Negative equity* is a term used to describe a home where more money is owed than the house is worth. For example if the first mortgage is $150,000 and the second mortgage from a home equity loan is $10,000, the total debt owed against the house is $160,000. If your home is valued at $140,000, the equity in your home is negative $20,000 (the $140,000 value less the $160,000 in mortgages equals negative $20,000 in equity). There is no

147

equity—there is just debt. To sell the house then would require that money be brought by the seller to the closing table.

11.7   How will the equity in our house be divided?

If your home is going to be sold, the equity in the home will most likely be divided (according to equitable division principles) at the time of the sale, after the costs of the sale have been paid.

If either you or your spouse will be awarded the house, there are a number of options for the other party being compensated the share of the equity in the marital home. These could include:

- The spouse who does not receive the house receives other assets (for example, retirement funds) to compensate for the value of the equity.
- The person who remains in the home agrees to refinance the home at some future date and to pay the other party the share of the equity.
- The parties agree that the property be sold at a future date, or upon the happening of a certain event such as the youngest child completing high school or the remarriage of the party keeping the home.

Because the residence is often among the most valuable assets considered in a divorce, it is important that you and your attorney discuss the details of its disposition. These include:

- Valuation of the property
- Refinancing to remove a party from liability for the mortgage
- The dates on which certain actions should be taken, such as listing the home for sale
- The real estate broker
- Costs of preparing the home for sale
- Making mortgage payments

If you and your spouse do not agree on which of you will remain in the home, the court (either the judge or jury) will decide who keeps it or may order the property sold.

11.8 What happens if we owe more than the house is worth?

Because of the housing market bust, there are more and more cases like this. If you owe more for your house than it's worth, then you need to discuss your options with your lawyer and discuss financial options with your lender.

These discussions should focus on:

- The value of the property
- The debt owed versus the value—how much is the "negative equity"?
- The chances of the value coming back or increasing
- The costs associated with moving
- Giving a deed to the lender in lieu of foreclosure
- Filing for bankruptcy protection
- Allowing the house to be foreclosed
- Short-sale opportunities
- Effect on your credit
- Modifications of the mortgage
- Making mortgage payments

11.9 Who keeps all the household goods until the decree is signed?

The court will ordinarily not make any decisions about who keeps the household goods on a temporary basis (although if there is something specific that needs to be addressed, then make it known to your lawyer and the matter can properly be resolved by the court). Most couples attempt to resolve these issues on their own rather than incur legal fees to dispute household goods on a temporary basis.

If certain items have to be divided, then the court will divide them on an equitable basis.

11.10 How are assets such as cars, boats, and furniture divided, and when does this happen?

In most cases spouses are able to reach their own agreements about how to divide personal property, such as household furnishings and vehicles.

If you and your spouse disagree about how to divide certain items, it can be wise to consider which are truly valuable to you, financially or otherwise. Perhaps some of the items can be easily replaced. Always look to see whether it is a good use of your attorney fees to argue over items of personal property. If a negotiated settlement cannot be reached, the issue of the division of your property will be made by the judge or jury at trial.

One technique that is sometimes used is having the parties list the property that they are disagreeing about and then allowing one party (usually the one that earns the least amount of money) to select an item from the list and then the other party selects an item—and this process continues until all the items are divided. Usually, if an item of personal property has a debt still owed on it, the debt will go with the property.

11.11 What is meant by a *property inventory* and how detailed should mine be?

A *property inventory* is a listing of the property owned. It may also include a brief description of the property and estimated value and debt owed on that item. Discuss with your attorney the level of inventory detail needed to benefit your case.

Factors to consider when creating your inventory may include:

- The extent to which you anticipate you and your spouse will disagree regarding the division of your property
- Whether you anticipate a dispute regarding the value of the property either you or your spouse is retaining
- Whether you will have continued access to the property if a later inventory is needed or whether your spouse will retain control of the property
- Whether you and your spouse are likely to disagree about which items are premarital, inherited, or gifts from someone other than your spouse

In addition to creating an inventory, your attorney may request that you prepare a list of the property that you and your spouse have already divided or a list of the items you want but your spouse has not agreed to give to you.

If you do not have continued access to your property, talk to your attorney about taking photographs of or obtaining access to the property to complete your inventory.

11.12 How and when are liquid assets like bank accounts and stocks divided?

Talk with your attorney early in your case about the benefits of a temporary restraining order to reduce the risk that your spouse will transfer money out of financial accounts or transfer other assets.

In many cases couples will agree to divide bank accounts equally at the outset of the case. However, this may not be advisable in your case. Discuss with your attorney whether you should keep an accounting of how you spend money used from a bank account while your divorce is in progress.

Stocks are ordinarily a part of the final agreement for the division of property and debts. If you and your spouse cannot agree on how your investments should be divided, the judge or jury will make the decision at trial.

The division of these assets will be according to equitable division.

11.13 How is pet custody determined?

Unfortunately, Georgia law currently views pets as mere personal property. Therefore, there are no pet-specific laws regarding custody of pets. Because pets are viewed as property, the judge or jury is likely to award the pet to one party. Factors that courts have considered include:

- Is the pet registered in the name of one of the spouses with an organization, such as the American Kennel Club for pedigreed dogs?

- Who has been the primary care provider for the pet?

- Are the veterinarian records for the pet in the name of only one spouse?

- Is only one spouse registered as owner by the local animal control department that is responsible for rabies vaccinations?

- Is only one spouse registered as owner in the microchip records (if the pet has been microchipped by a veterinarian) or registered with an organization that helps reunite a lost pet with an owner (such as Home Again).

- Who will best be able to meet the pet's daily needs for companionship, nurturing, training, feeding, walking, medical care, and affection?

If the parties can reach an agreement outside court, then it's possible that such an agreement would be upheld by the court under the same rules as for other contracts. These types of agreements (sometimes referred to as *pet custody agreements*) allow for:

- Specific periods of time to be spent with the pet
- The right to care for the pet when the other person is not able to
- The right to be informed of the pet's health

If it is important to you to be awarded one of your family pets, discuss the matter with your attorney. It may be possible to reach a pet-care agreement with your spouse that will allow you to share possession and responsibility for your pets.

11.14 How will our property in another state be divided?

For the purposes of dividing your assets, out-of-state property is treated the same as property in Georgia. Although a Georgia court cannot order a change in the title to property located in another state, a judge can order your spouse either to turn the property over to you or to sign a deed or other document to transfer title to you.

11.15 I worked like a dog for years to support my family while my spouse completed an advanced degree. Do I have a right to any of my spouse's future earnings?

Your contributions during the marriage are a factor to be considered in both the division of the property and debts, as well as any award of alimony. Be sure to give your attorney a complete history of your contributions to the marriage and ask about their impact on the outcome of your case.

11.16 Are all of the assets I owned prior to this marriage—such as property, bank accounts, and inheritances—still going to be solely mine after the divorce?

It depends. In many cases the court will allow a party to retain an asset brought into the marriage (also known as *separate* or *premarital property*), but the following are questions the court will consider in making its determination:

- Can the premarital asset be clearly traced? For example, if you continue to own a vehicle that you brought into the marriage, it is likely that it will be awarded to you. However, if you brought a vehicle into the marriage, sold it during the marriage, and spent the proceeds, it is unlikely that the court will consider awarding you its value. However, if the vehicle was traded in for a replacement vehicle, then maybe you would get some portion of the value of the new vehicle awarded as premarital property.

- Did you keep the property separate and titled in your name, or did you commingle it with marital assets? Premarital assets you kept separate and did not commingle will likely be awarded to you.

- Did the other spouse contribute to the increase in the value of the premarital asset, and can the value of that increase be proven? For example, suppose a woman owned a home prior to her marriage. After the marriage, the parties live in the home, continuing to make mortgage payments and improvements to the home. At the time of the divorce, the husband seeks a portion of the equity in the home. The court might consider the value of the home at the time of the marriage, any contributions to the increase in equity made by the husband, and the evidence of the value of those contributions.

The laws regarding marital assets and separate assets is constantly evolving in Georgia. If these issues are expected in your divorce, then you should discuss the specifics with your lawyer.

11.17 Will I get to keep my engagement ring?

If your engagement ring was given to you prior to marriage (with no strings attached), it might be considered a gift and treated as separate property that you can keep. However, some courts have considered the ring as part of the marital property and distributed it according to equitable division.

11.18 Can I keep gifts and inheritances I received during the marriage?

Similar rules apply to gifts and inheritances received during the marriage as apply to premarital assets, that is, assets you owned prior to the marriage.

Gifts that you and your spouse gave to one another may be treated as any other marital asset. For gifts received from others during the marriage, such as a gift from a parent, the court will need to determine whether the gift was made to one party or to both. Whether you will be entitled to keep assets you inherited, assuming they are still in existence, will depend upon the unique circumstances of your case. When dividing the marital estate, the court may consider the fact that one spouse is allowed to keep substantial nonmarital assets such as an inheritance.

The following factors increase the probability that you will be entitled to keep your inheritance:

- It has been kept separate from the marital assets, such as in a separate account.
- It is titled in your name only.
- It can be clearly identified.
- It has not been commingled with marital assets.
- Your spouse has not contributed to its care, operation, or improvement.

It is less likely that you will be awarded your full inheritance if the following factors have occurred:

- It was commingled with marital assets.
- Its origin cannot be traced.
- You have placed your spouse's name on the title.
- Your spouse has contributed to the increase in the value of the inheritance.

If keeping your inheritance is important to you, talk to your attorney about the information needed to build your case. If you are likely to receive an inheritance or a substantial gift, then discuss with your lawyer the best way to try to keep this asset your separate property.

11.19 If my spouse and I can't decide who gets what property, who divides the property between us? If one of us is unhappy with that decision, can it be appealed?

If you and your spouse cannot agree on the division of your property, the court will make a judgment after considering the evidence at your trial. In Georgia, a judge will be the decision maker, unless either party demands a jury trial instead. If either party is dissatisfied with the decision reached by the judge (or jury), an appeal to a higher court is possible.

Georgia is an equitable ("what is fair and reasonable") division state. So, if the assets are divided equitably then the chances of succeeding on an appeal are slim. Therefore, a cost-benefit analysis is appropriate. If you're unhappy over not getting a $1,000 item, you might think twice before investing $3,000 to appeal, when the odds may be against success.

It's usually better to try to reach an agreement regarding the division of personal property rather than chance the risky outcome of an appeal because you never know what the judge or jury will do. More than likely no one is going to be happy about having to decide who gets the bedroom TV and who gets the living room TV. Also, is what you are fighting over worth the time, money, and stress that it will take to fight over it?

11.20 What is a *property settlement agreement*?

A *property settlement agreement* is a written document that includes all of the financial agreements you and your spouse have reached in your divorce. This may include the division of property, debts, child support, alimony, insurance, and attorney fees.

The property settlement may be a separate document, or it may be incorporated into the final decree of divorce, which is the final court order dissolving your marriage.

This agreement is usually the contract that controls the terms of your divorce. Although these agreements are often made in the order of the court as part of the divorce, they are oftentimes still enforceable under contract rules even if they are not made by the order of the court.

11.21   How are the values of property determined?

The value of some assets, like bank accounts, are usually not disputed. The value of other assets, such as homes or personal property, are more likely to be disputed.

If your case proceeds to trial, you may give your opinion of the value of property you own. You or your spouse may also have certain property appraised by an expert. In such cases it may be necessary to have the appraiser appear at trial to give testimony regarding the appraisal and the value of the asset.

If you own substantial assets for which the value is likely to be disputed, talk to your attorney early in your case about the benefits and costs of expert witnesses.

11.22   What does *date of valuation* mean?

Because the value of assets can go up or down while a divorce is pending, it can be necessary to determine a set date for valuing the marital assets. This is referred to as the *date of valuation*. You and your spouse can agree on what date the assets should be valued. If you cannot agree, the judge or jury will decide the date of valuation.

Among the most common dates used are the date of separation, the date of the filing of the divorce complaint, or the date of the divorce trial.

11.23   What happens after my spouse and I approve the property settlement agreement? Do we still have to go to court?

After you and your spouse sign your names to approve the property settlement agreement or decree, it must still be approved by the judge. Some courts will require at least one party to attend a final uncontested hearing where that party will "prove the divorce" (present evidence). However, some courts will allow you to prove the divorce through a written affidavit so that your presence is not required. Discuss these options with your attorney.

Assuming you and your spouse have also resolved all matters pertaining to your minor children and all issues in your divorce, the court will allow you to schedule this final un-contested hearing any time after forty-five days from the time the defendant received notice of the divorce. (If you and your spouse agree, the court will waive fifteen days and therefore, you will be required to wait only thirty days from the proof of service or acknowledgment to finalize the divorce.)

If a property settlement agreement is reached by the par-ties, a court date for your final hearing can often be obtained earlier than a trial date because a final uncontested hearing requires much less time than a trial.

11.24 If my spouse and I think our property settlement agreement is fair, why does the judge have to approve it?

The judge has a duty to review all property settlement agreements in divorces. For this reason, the judge must review your agreement. The judge can consider the facts and circum-stances of your case when reviewing the agreement. Not every case will result in an equal division of the assets and debts from the marriage, although equal division is not uncommon.

11.25 What happens to our individual checking and savings accounts during and after the divorce?

Regardless of whose name is on the account, bank ac-counts may be considered marital assets and may be divided by the court. The same rules for marital and nonmarital prop-erty govern this division.

Discuss with your attorney the benefits of a temporary restraining order to protect bank accounts, how to use these accounts while the case is pending, and the date on which financial accounts should be valued.

11.26 Who gets the interest from certificates of deposit, dividends from stock holdings, and so on, during the divorce proceedings?

Whether you or your spouse receive interest from these assets is decided as a part of the overall division of your property and debts. It will be divided based on equitable division.

11.27 Do each one of our financial accounts have to be divided in half if we agree to an equal division of our assets?

No. Rather than incurring the administrative challenges and expense of dividing each asset in half, you and your spouse can decide that one of you will take certain assets equal to the value of assets taken by the spouse. If necessary, one of you can agree to make a cash payment to the other to make an equitable division. It is important to remember that equitable division does not necessarily mean 50/50. This is why it is important to discuss the division of assets with your attorney.

11.28 What factors determine whether I can get at least half of my spouse's business?

Many factors determine whether you will get a share of your spouse's business and in what form you might receive it. Among the factors the court will look at are:

- Whether your spouse owned the business prior to your marriage
- Your role, if any, in operating the business or increasing its value
- The overall division of the property and debts

If you or your spouse own a business, it is important that you work with your attorney early in your case to develop a strategy for valuing the business and making your case for how it should be treated in the division of property and debts.

11.29 My spouse and I have owned and run our own business together for many years. Can I be forced out of it?

Deciding what should happen with a family business when divorce occurs can be a challenge. Because of the risk for future conflict between you and your spouse, the value of the business is likely to be substantially decreased if you both remain owners.

In discussing your options with your attorney, consider the following questions:

- If one spouse retains ownership of the business, are there enough other assets for the other spouse to receive a fair share of the total marital assets?
- Which spouse has the skills and experience to continue running the business?
- What would you do if you weren't working in the business?
- What is the value of the business?
- What is the market for the business if it were to be sold?
- Could you remain an employee of the business for some period of time even if you were not an owner?

You and your spouse know your business best. With the help of your lawyers, you may be able to create a settlement that can satisfy you both. If not, the judge or jury will make the decision for you at trial.

11.30 I suspect my spouse is hiding assets, but I can't prove it. How can I protect myself if I discover later that I was right?

Ask your attorney to include language in your divorce decree to address your concern. Insist that it include an acknowledgment by your spouse that the agreement was based upon a full and complete disclosure of your spouse's financial condition. Discuss with your attorney a provision that allows for setting aside the agreement if it is later discovered that assets were hidden.

If your spouse is not honest while under oath, then discuss this perjury and fraud with your lawyer and discuss the possibility of overturning the divorce based on that fraud.

11.31 My spouse and I are farmers. What do I need to know about dividing our assets?

Dividing the value of farm operations can be complex because of the many sources of income and debts. Look for an attorney experienced in farm divorces and familiar with the *Federal Farm Bill* on federal funding for farmers.

These are the actions that might be needed in your case:

- Sending copies of your temporary restraining order regarding property to financial institutions, major customers, or agencies that might be involved with the transfer of farm assets

- Conducting more in-depth discovery in order to get information such as the timing of payments, contracts, agreements to withhold payment, prepurchased feed or fertilizer, and grain delivered but not receipted

- Obtaining information under the *Freedom of Information Act (FOIA)* from federal agencies such as the Department of Agriculture or the Farm Credit Administration

- Using a forensic accountant to help investigate, including evaluating balance sheets and tracing cash flow

Work closely with your attorney to be sure that you have a complete and accurate picture of your financial situation before entering settlement negotiations or proceeding to trial.

11.32 My spouse says I'm not entitled to a share of his stock options because they are lost if his employment is terminated with the company. What are my rights?

Stock options are often a very valuable asset. They are also one of the most complex issues when dividing assets during a divorce for these and other reasons:

- Each company has its own rules about awarding and exercising stock options.

- Complete information is needed from the employer.

- There are different methods for calculating the value of stock options.

- The reasons the options were given can impact the valuation. For example, some are given for future performance.

- There are cost and tax considerations when options are exercised.

Rather than being awarded a portion of the stock options themselves, you are likely to receive a share of the proceeds when the stock options are exercised.

If either you or your spouse owns stock options, begin discussing this asset with your attorney early in your case to allow sufficient time to settle the issues or to be well prepared for trial.

11.33 What is a *prenuptial agreement* and how might it affect the property settlement phase of the divorce?

A *prenuptial agreement,* sometimes referred to as a *premarital agreement,* is a contract entered into between two people prior to their marriage. It can include provisions for how assets and debts will be divided in the event the marriage is terminated, as well as terms concerning child support or alimony.

Your property settlement is likely to be impacted by the terms of your prenuptial agreement if the agreement is upheld as valid by the court.

11.34 Can a prenuptial agreement be contested during the divorce?

Yes. The court may consider many factors in determining whether to uphold your prenuptial agreement. Among them are:

- Whether your agreement was entered into voluntarily
- Whether your agreement was fair and reasonable at the time it was signed
- Whether you and your spouse each gave a complete disclosure of your assets and debts
- Whether you and your spouse each had your own attorney
- Whether you and your spouse each had enough time to consider the agreement

If you have a prenuptial agreement, take a copy of it to the initial consultation with your attorney. Be sure to provide your attorney with a detailed history of the facts and circumstances surrounding reaching and signing the agreement.

11.35 I've heard the old saying "Possession is nine-tenths of the law." Is that true during divorce proceedings?

It can be. Consulting with an attorney before the filing of divorce can reduce the risk that assets will be hidden, transferred, or destroyed by your spouse. This is especially important if your spouse has a history of destroying property, incurring substantial debt, or transferring money without your knowledge.

Among possible actions you and your attorney can consider together include:

- Placing your family heirlooms or other valuables in a safe location
- Transferring some portion of financial accounts prior to filing for divorce
- Preparing an inventory of the personal property
- Taking photographs or a video of the property
- Obtaining copies of important financial records or statements
- Obtaining a restraining order before your spouse is served with notice of the divorce

Plans to leave the marital home should also be discussed in detail with your attorney, so that any actions taken early in your case are consistent with your ultimate goals.

Speak candidly with your attorney about your concerns so that a plan that provides a level of protection appropriate to your circumstances can be developed.

11.36 I'm Jewish and need my spouse to cooperate with obtaining a *get*, which is a divorce document under our religion. Can I get a court order to require my spouse to consent to the *get*?

No. Talk to your attorney about obtaining a *get* cooperation clause in your settlement agreement, if any, including a provision regarding who should pay for it. At this time, the law regarding this has not been established in Georgia.

11.37 Who will get the mother's frozen egg or embryo, and the father's sperm that we have stored at the health clinic?

The law on this issue is not yet fully established in Georgia. The terms of your contract with the clinic may impact the rights you and your spouse may have to the egg, the embryo, and the sperm, so provide a copy of the contract to your attorney for review. If permissible under your contract, you and your spouse may want to consider donating the embryo to another couple.

11.38 Will debts be considered when determining the division of the property?

Yes. The court will consider the marital debts when dividing the property. For example, if you are awarded a car valued at $12,000, but you owe a $10,000 debt on the same vehicle, the court will take that debt into consideration in the overall division of the assets that you are getting a $2,000 car—not a $12,000 car—because the debt should be subtracted from its value. Similarly, if one spouse agrees to pay substantial marital credit card debt, this obligation may also be considered in the final determination of the division of property and debts.

If your spouse incurred debts that you believe should not be your responsibility, tell your attorney. Some debts may be considered nonmarital and treated separately from other debts incurred during the marriage. For example, if your spouse spent large sums of money on gambling or illegal drugs without your knowledge, you may be able to argue that those debts should be the sole responsibility of your spouse.

11.39 What happens to the property distribution if one of us dies before the divorce proceedings are completed?

If your spouse dies prior to your divorce decree being entered, you will generally be considered married and treated as a surviving spouse under the law. However, every case is different and depends on the particular facts and circumstances of your case. The laws of *probate* governing wills and distribution of estates will control, unless you both entered into a binding settlement or separate maintenance agreement.

12

Benefits: Insurance, Retirement, and Pensions

Divorce: Freedom with strings attached

During your marriage, you might have taken certain employment benefits for granted. You might not have given much thought each month to having health, or medical, insurance through your spouse's work. When you find yourself in a divorce, suddenly these benefits come to the forefront of your mind.

You might also, even unconsciously, have seen your own employment retirement benefits as belonging to you and not your spouse, referring to "my 401(k)" or "my pension." After all, you are the one who went to work every day to earn it, right?

When you divorce, some benefits arising from your spouse's employment will end, some may continue for a period of time, and others may be divided between you. Retirement funds, in particular, are often one of the most valuable marital assets that may be divided in a divorce.

Whether the benefits are from your employer or your spouse's, with your attorney's help you will develop a better understanding of which benefits the law considers to be "mine," "yours," or "ours" for continuing or dividing.

12.1 Will our children continue to have health coverage through my spouse's work even though we're divorcing?

If either you or your spouse currently provides health insurance for your children, it is very likely that the court will order the insurance to remain in place for as long as it remains available and support is being paid for your child.

The cost of insurance for the children will be taken into consideration in determining the amount of child support to be paid.

12.2 Will I continue to have health insurance through my spouse's work after the divorce?

It depends. If your spouse currently provides health insurance for you, you may be treated as a spouse for health insurance purposes for a period of time following the entry of your divorce decree. However, some health insurance policies exclude spousal coverage after thirty days from the entry of the divorce decree. Some health insurance policies even terminate coverage as of entry of the final judgment and decree of divorce.

Investigate the cost of continuing on your spouse's employer-provided plans under a federal law known as *COBRA*. This coverage can be maintained for up to three years. However, the cost can be very high, so you will want to determine whether it's a realistic option.

Tell your attorney if you want or need to be kept on your spouse's health insurance policy. If you have no other health insurance, this is an important provision to be included in your divorce decree. If it is not possible to remain on your spouse's health insurance, then you might consider the price of a private policy or a policy through your employment and possibly seek to have your spouse pay for it.

Begin early to investigate your options for your future health insurance. The cost of your health care is an important factor when pursuing spousal support and planning your post-divorce budget.

12.3 How many years must I have been married before I'm eligible to receive a part of my spouse's retirement fund or pension?

There is no magic number. Even if your marriage is not of long duration, you may be entitled to a portion of your spouse's retirement fund or pension accumulated during the marriage. For example, if you were married for three years and your spouse contributed $10,000 to a 401(k) plan during the marriage, it is possible that the court would award you 100 percent of the value of the contribution when dividing your property and debts. It is also possible that you could receive 0 percent of the value. Although neither one of these scenarios is likely, they are possible and illustrate the uncertainties of an equitable distribution of property.

There are many factors that should be considered when determining equitable division of property. The dividing of retirement accounts and pension plans is governed by the rules of equitable division.

12.4 I contributed to my pension plan for ten years before I got married. Will my spouse get half of my entire pension?

Probably not. It is more likely the court will award your spouse only a portion of your retirement that was acquired during the marriage.

If either you or your spouse made premarital contributions to a pension or retirement plan, be sure to let your attorney know. This is information essential to determine which portion of the retirement plan should be treated as premarital and thus unlikely to be shared. But you should keep in mind the rules regarding commingling money and making a premarital asset a marital asset. The answer to this question will rely heavily on how the money is traced.

12.5 I plan to keep my same job after my divorce. Will my former spouse get half of the money I contribute to my retirement plan after my divorce?

No. Your former spouse should be entitled to only a portion of your retirement that was accumulated during the marriage. Talk with your attorney so that the language of the court order ensures protection of your postdivorce retirement contributions.

12.6 Am I still entitled to a share of my spouse's retirement even though I never contributed to one during our twenty-five-year marriage?

Probably. Retirements are often the most valuable asset accumulated during a marriage. Consequently, your judge or jury should consider the retirement along with all of the other marital assets and debts when determining an equitable division. It is important to remember that most property, with a few exceptions, acquired during the marriage will be considered marital property.

12.7 I have been told I will be getting a share of my spouse's retirement. How can I find out how much I get and when I'm eligible to receive it?

A number of factors will determine your rights to collect from your spouse's retirement. One factor will be the terms of the court order dividing the retirement. The court order will tell you whether you are entitled to a set dollar amount, a percentage, or a fraction to be determined based upon the length of your marriage and how long your spouse continues working.

Another factor will be the terms of the retirement plan itself. Some provide for lump-sum withdrawals; others will issue payments only in monthly installments. Review both the terms of your court order and contact the plan administrator to obtain the clearest understanding of your rights and benefits.

12.8 If I am eligible to receive my spouse's retirement benefits, do I have to be sixty-five to collect them?

It depends upon the terms of your spouse's retirement plan. In some cases it is possible to begin receiving your share at the earliest date your former spouse is eligible to receive them, regardless of whether your former spouse elects to do so. Check the terms of your spouse's plan to learn your options.

12.9 What happens if my former spouse is old enough to receive benefits but I'm not?

Ordinarily you will be eligible to begin receiving your share of the benefits when your former spouse begins receiving benefits. Depending upon the plan, you may be eligible to receive them sooner. The right to receive benefits will often be controlled by the plan. Specific questions should be directed to the plan administrator.

12.10 Am I entitled to cost-of-living increases on my share of my spouse's retirement?

It depends. If your spouse has a retirement plan that includes a provision for a *cost-of-living allowance (COLA)*, talk to your attorney about whether this can be included in the court order dividing the retirement.

12.11 What circumstances might prevent me from getting part of my spouse's retirement benefits?

Some pension plans are not subject to division (such as some government plans). If you or your spouse are employed by a government agency or your pension plan is not subject to division, talk with your attorney about how this may affect the property settlement in your case. Also, retirement plans are like other marital property and governed by the rules of equitable division. So, even if the plan does not allow for division, it is possible that the court will find other ways to make the division equitable, such as an award of other assets to make up for the difference.

12.12 Does the death of my spouse affect the payout of retirement benefits to me or to our children?

It depends upon both the nature of your spouse's retirement plan and the terms of the court order dividing the retirement. Discuss this issue with your attorney before your case is settled or goes to trial.

Some plans allow only a surviving spouse or former spouse to be a beneficiary. Others may allow for the naming of an alternate beneficiary, such as the children.

12.13 How can I be sure I'll get my share of my former spouse's retirement when I am entitled to it years from now?

Rather than relying upon your former spouse to pay you your share of a future retirement, your best protection is a court order that provides for the retirement or pension plan administrator to pay the money directly to you. This type of court order is often referred to as a *qualified domestic relations order (QDRO)*. These orders help ensure that a nonemployee spouse receives his or her share directly from the employee spouse's plan.

Obtaining a QDRO is a critical step in the divorce process. They can be complex documents, and a number of steps are required to reduce future concerns about enforcement and fully protect your rights. These court orders must comply with numerous technical rules and be approved by the plan administrator, which is often located outside Georgia.

Whenever possible, the QDRO or other court order dividing retirement plans should be entered at the same time as the decree of dissolution. Of course, the plan administrator will not pay out benefits if unaware of the court order—so ensure the order is submitted by certified mail or other delivery service that provides proof of receipt.

12.14 If my former spouse dies before I do, can I still collect on the Social Security account of the decedent?

It depends. If you were married to your spouse for ten or more years and you have not remarried, you may be eligible for benefits. Contact your local Social Security Administration (SSA) office or visit the SSA website at www.ssa.gov. If you have questions about Social Security, it is important to discuss these with a Social Security–savvy attorney.

12.15 What orders might the court enter regarding life insurance?

The judge may order you or your spouse to maintain a life insurance policy to ensure that future support payments are made. In most cases you will be required to pay for your own life insurance after your divorce, and you should include this as an expense in your monthly budget.

It is important to note that if you are maintaining a life insurance policy for the benefit of the children, then you can request a deviation/deduction from your child-support obligation based upon that monthly insurance premium. The Georgia child-support worksheets have a specific place for this deviation.

12.16 Because we share children, should I consider my spouse as a beneficiary on my life insurance?

It depends upon your intentions. If your intention is to give the money to your former spouse, by all means name the other parent as beneficiary.

However, if you intend the life insurance proceeds to be used for the benefit of your children, talk with your attorney about your options. Georgia law and the probate court may prevent the insurance funds payable to the child as beneficiary from being used to support or educate that child because those funds are legally the child's own property, and the surviving parent has the legal obligation to provide support and education from the parent's own money.

You may consider naming a trustee to manage the life insurance proceeds on behalf of your children, and there may be reasons to choose someone other than your former spouse (such as a grandparent or other relative).

12.17 Can the court require in the decree that I be the beneficiary of my spouse's insurance policy, as long as the children are minors or indefinitely?

Generally, yes. When a court order is entered for life insurance, it is ordinarily for the purposes of ensuring payment of future support and will terminate when the support obligation has ended. If the purpose of the life insurance is to ensure child support, then the order will likely specify this and could include language about the money being used for the child's support. However, as noted earlier, Georgia law and the probate court may prevent the insurance funds payable to the child as beneficiary from being used to support or educate that child because those funds are legally the child's own property, and the surviving parent has the legal obligation to provide support and education from the parent's own money.

13

Division of Debts

A mountain of debt is conquered the same way as the real mountain—one step at a time.

Throughout a marriage, most couples will have disagreements about money from time to time. You might think extra money should be spent on a family vacation, and your spouse might insist it should be saved for retirement. You might think it's time you finally get a new car, and your spouse thinks you would be fine driving the ten-year-old van for two more years.

If you and your spouse had different philosophies about saving and spending during your marriage, chances are you will have very differing opinions when dividing your debts in divorce. What you both can count on is that Georgia law provides that, to reach a fair outcome, the payment of debts must also be taken into consideration when dividing the assets from your marriage.

There are steps you can take to ensure the best outcome possible when it comes to dividing your marital debt. These include providing accurate and complete debt information to your attorney and asking your attorney to include provisions in your divorce decree to protect you in the future if your spouse refuses to pay his or her share.

Regardless of how the debts from your marriage are divided, know that you will have the opportunity to gradually build your independent financial success when making a fresh start after your divorce is final, no matter how difficult it may seem.

13.1 Who is responsible for paying credit card bills and making house payments during the divorce proceedings?

In some cases the court will make decisions regarding the payment of credit card debt on a temporary basis. It is important to work with your attorney and your spouse to reach a temporary agreement regarding these debts because you may not like the judge's temporary decision. Discuss the importance of making at least minimum payments on time to avoid substantial finance charges and late fees.

If there is not a court order or an agreement between the parties, then the default position would be that whoever's name is on the debt will owe the payment; if both names are on the debt then the debt is likely owed by both parties. However, this default position relies on both parties being financially equal.

Often, the spouse who remains in the home will be responsible for the mortgage payments, taxes, utilities, and most other ordinary home expenses, but few judges will order the impossible if that spouse cannot realistically handle the expenses.

If you are concerned that you cannot afford to stay in the marital home on a temporary basis, talk with your attorney about your options prior to your temporary hearing.

13.2 What, if anything, should I be doing with the credit card companies as we go through the divorce?

If possible, it is best to obtain some separate credit prior to the divorce. This will help you establish credit in your own name and help you with necessary purchases following a separation.

Begin by obtaining a copy of your credit report from at least two of the three nationwide consumer reporting companies: Experian, Equifax, and TransUnion. The Fair Credit Reporting Act entitles you a free copy of your credit report from each of these three companies every twelve months.

To order your free annual report online, go to www.annualcreditreport.com, call toll-free to (877) 322-8228, or complete an Annual Credit Report Request Form and mail it to: Annual Credit Report Request Service, P.O. Box 105281, Atlanta,

GA 30348-5281. You can print the form from the Federal Trade Commission website at www.ftc.gov. Your spouse may have incurred debt using your name. This information is important to relay to your attorney. If you and your spouse have joint credit card accounts, contact each credit card company to determine if you can close the account or limit your obligation for future charges on that account. Do the same if you are the primary cardholder and your spouse is an authorized user on your account.

If you want to maintain credit with a company, ask to have a new account in your own name. Be sure to let your spouse know (or provide advance notice) if you close an account being used by the spouse, especially if the welfare of children would be jeopardized.

13.3   How is credit card debt divided?

Credit card debt will be divided as a part of the overall division of the marital property and debts. Just as in the division of property, the court considers what is equitable, or fair, in your case.

If your spouse has exclusively used a credit card for purposes that did not benefit the family, such as gambling or entertaining a paramour, talk with your attorney. In most cases the court will not review a lengthy history of how you and your spouse used the credit cards, but there can be exceptions.

13.4   Am I responsible for repayment of my spouse's student loans?

Generally, no, but it is within the realm of possibility. If your spouse incurred student loans prior to the marriage, it is most likely that the student-borrower will be ordered to pay that debt.

If the debt was incurred during the marriage, how the funds were used may have an impact on who is ordered to pay them. For example, if your spouse borrowed $3,000 during the marriage for tuition, it is likely your spouse will be ordered to pay that debt. However, if a $3,000 student loan was taken out by your spouse, but $1,000 of it was used for the family living expenses or a family vacation, then the court would be more likely to order the debt shared.

The court may also consider payment on student loan debt when calculating the amount of support to be paid.

If you were a joint borrower on your spouse's student loan and your spouse fails to pay the loan, the lender may attempt to collect from you (even if your spouse has been ordered to pay). You are legally liable to the lender on that debt because you signed the loan contract in which you promised the lender you would pay. Although the judge may order the other spouse to pay the entire debt, the judge cannot take your name or obligation off the loan itself, so the lender may still demand you be responsible for the debt. Small consolation comes from the right you would have to seek reimbursement (indemnification) from your spouse if you were financially able to pay and did so to protect your credit rating. You may seek a finding of contempt, but realize if the spouse is judgment-proof, files for bankruptcy on the debt, or is just a deadbeat, there is no easy or swift relief.

If either you or your spouse has student loan debt, be sure to give your attorney the complete history regarding the debt and ask about possible outcomes under the facts of your case.

13.5 During the divorce proceedings, am I still responsible for debt my spouse continues to accrue?

Maybe. In most cases the court will order each of the parties to be responsible for each one's own post-separation debts. However, the strict rule of law in Georgia is that anything that is acquired up until the date of divorce can be considered marital property. That means that debts accrued during the separation might also be considered marital debts. If the post-separation debts are classified as marital debts, then your argument shifts to the equitable division of those debts.

13.6 During the marriage my spouse applied for and received several credit cards without my knowledge. Am I responsible for them?

Maybe. The court will consider the overall fairness of the property and debt division when deciding who should pay this debt. If your spouse bought items with the cards and intends to keep those items, it is likely that you will not be ordered to pay the debt incurred for those purchases.

If your name is not on the credit card account, then the credit card companies may not be able to pursue collection from you for the debt. But if your name is on the account, either as a joint cardholder or an authorized user, then these debts certainly need to be addressed in your divorce. The best advice is to always address any outstanding debt even if you think you have no obligation for it.

If you are concerned that your spouse is not going to pay the debts, then discuss this with your attorney and ask that precautions be taken for this, like the addition of a "hold-harmless" clause and provision for indemnification.

13.7 Regarding debts, what is a *hold-harmless* clause, and why should it be in the divorce decree?

A *hold-harmless* provision is intended to protect you in the event that your spouse fails to follow a court order to pay a debt after the divorce is granted. The language typically provides that your spouse shall "indemnify and hold (you) harmless from liability" on the debt. *Indemnification* means, if you pay, you are to be reimbursed.

If you and your spouse have a joint debt and your spouse fails to pay, the creditor may nevertheless attempt to collect from you. This is because the court is without power to change the creditor's rights. The judge has power to issue orders affecting only you and your spouse, not a creditor.

In the event your spouse fails to pay a court-ordered debt and the creditor attempts collection from you, the hold-harmless clause and indemnification provision in your divorce decree can be used in an effort to insist that payment is made by your former spouse and, if you pay due to demands of the creditor, you may seek reimbursement.

13.8 During our marriage, we paid off thousands of dollars of debt incurred by my spouse before we were married. Will the court take this into consideration when dividing our property and debt?

It might. Just as premarital assets can have an impact on the overall division of property and debts, so can premarital debt. Depending upon the length of the marriage, the evidence of the debt, and the amount paid, it may be a factor for the judge to consider.

Be sure to let your attorney know if either you or your spouse brought substantial debt into the marriage.

13.9 Why do my former spouse's doctors say they have a legal right to collect from me when my former spouse was ordered to pay those medical bills?

Your divorce decree does not take away the legal rights of creditors to collect debts. Contact your attorney about your right to enforce the court order that your spouse pay his or her own medical bills.

13.10 My spouse and I have agreed that I will keep our home; why must I refinance the mortgage?

There may be a number of reasons why your spouse is asking you to refinance the mortgage. First, the mortgage company cannot be forced to remove your spouse's name and obligation off the mortgage note. This means that if you did not make the house payments, the lender could pursue collection against your spouse.

Second, your spouse may not want to wait to receive his or her share of the home equity. It may be possible for you to borrow additional money at the time of refinancing to pay your spouse his or her share of the equity in the home.

Third, the mortgage on your family home may prevent your spouse from buying a home in the future. Because all existing debt obligations are counted in determining credit risk, and there remains a possibility that your spouse could be pursued for the debt to the mortgage company, it is unlikely that a second lender will want to take the risk of extending further credit to your spouse.

It is important to note that in some limited cases the mortgage lender will allow the party keeping the home to "assume the mortgage" and remove the other party's name. This process is cheaper and less involved than a refinance. By assuming sole responsibility for the mortgage, the party who stays on the mortgage debt removes the other party's liability for that mortgage debt. This option should be discussed with your lawyer and your lender to see if it is appropriate in your situation.

13.11 Can I file for bankruptcy while my divorce is pending?

Consult with your attorney if you are considering filing for bankruptcy while your divorce is pending. It will be important for you to ask yourself a number of questions, such as:

- Should I file for bankruptcy on my own or with my spouse?
- How will my filing for bankruptcy affect my ability to purchase a home in the future?
- Which debts can be discharged in bankruptcy, and which cannot?
- How will a bankruptcy affect the division of property and debts in the divorce?
- How might a delay in the divorce proceedings due to a bankruptcy impact my case?
- Which form of bankruptcy is best for my situation?

If you are represented by one attorney for the bankruptcy and another attorney for the divorce (which is common due to the specialized nature of bankruptcy practice), be sure that each attorney is kept fully informed about the developments in the other case.

13.12 What happens if my spouse files for bankruptcy during our divorce?

Contact your attorney right away. The filing of a bankruptcy stops the divorce action, and Federal Court approval to proceed is required before the divorce action may continue, except as to establishing child support and alimony. Bankruptcy while your divorce is pending obviously can have a significant impact on your divorce. Your attorney can advise you whether certain debts are likely to be discharged in the bankruptcy, the delay a bankruptcy may cause to your divorce, and whether bankruptcy is an appropriate option for you.

13.13   Can I file for divorce while I am in bankruptcy?

Yes, however, you must receive the bankruptcy court's approval with the divorce. While in bankruptcy, your property is protected from debt collection by the automatic stay. The stay can also prevent the divorce court from dividing property between you and your spouse until you obtain the bankruptcy court's permission to proceed with the divorce. However, under the current bankruptcy rules an action to establish child support and spousal support can proceed without permission. It is important to discuss this with your attorney before any action is taken because there are strict rules regarding violations of an automatic stay of a bankruptcy.

13.14   What should I do if my former spouse files for bankruptcy after our divorce?

Contact your attorney immediately. If you learn that your former spouse has filed for bankruptcy, you may have certain rights to object to the discharge of any debts your spouse was ordered to pay under your divorce decree. If you fail to take action, it is possible that you will be barred from getting what was awarded in the divorce and you may be held responsible for debts your spouse was ordered to pay.

14

Taxes

In this world nothing can be said to be certain,
except death and taxes.
    –Benjamin Franklin

Nobody likes a surprise letter from the Internal Revenue Service saying you owe more taxes and warning that the IRS may seize your property, seize or freeze all your bank accounts, and garnish your wages. When your divorce is over, you want to be sure that you don't later discover you owe taxes you weren't expecting to pay.

A number of tax issues may arise in your divorce. Your attorney may not be able to answer all of your tax questions, so it is always important to consult with your accountant or tax advisor for additional information.

Taxes are important considerations in both settlement negotiations and trial preparation. They should not be overlooked. Taxes can impact many of your decisions including those involving alimony, division of property, and the receipt of benefits.

Be sure to ask the professionals helping you about the tax implications in your divorce so you don't get that letter in the mail that begins, "Dear Taxpayer:..."

14.1 Will either my spouse or I have to pay income tax when we transfer property or pay a property settlement to each other according to our divorce decree?

Generally, no. However, it is important that you plan for the future tax consequences of a subsequent withdrawal, sale, or transfer of certain assets you receive in your divorce.

It is important to ask your tax advisor about potential consequences and to discuss these consequences with your attorney.

14.2 Is the amount of child support I pay tax deductible?

No, it is neither deductible by the payor not taxable as income to the payee/recipient.

14.3 Do I have to pay income tax on any child support I receive?

No, it is neither taxable as income for the payee/receiver, nor deductible by the payor.

14.4 Is the amount of alimony I am ordered to pay tax deductible?

Maybe. Generally, alimony as spousal support is tax deductible for the payor and taxable to the payee/receiver. This will include court-ordered alimony and may also include other forms of spousal support, but child support is not deductible. However, Georgia has specific rules regarding lump-sum alimony and periodic alimony. The best advice is to have any agreement specify if the money is to be treated as deductible or not, and confer with your accountant.

Your tax deduction is a factor to consider when determining a fair amount of alimony to be paid in your case. Both spouses should treat the alimony the same: either as deductible for the payor and taxable for the receiver, or not. If the IRS sees a discrepancy between the two spouses, at least one party is going to get audited or receive that Notice of Taxes Due.

14.5 Do I have to pay tax on the alimony I receive?

Generally, the answer is yes, you must pay income tax on the spousal support you receive. This will include court-ordered alimony and may also include other forms of spousal support, but not child support, paid by your spouse. However, Georgia has specific rules regarding lump-sum alimony and periodic alimony. The best advice is to have any agreement specify if the money is to be treated as taxable or not.

Income tax is a critical factor in determining a fair amount of alimony. Insist that your attorney bring this issue to the attention of your spouse's attorney or to the judge, if your case proceeds to trial, so that both the tax you pay and the deduction your spouse receives are taken into consideration.

Be sure to consult with your tax advisor about payment of tax on your spousal support. Making estimated tax payments throughout the year or withholding additional taxes from your wages can avoid a burdensome tax liability at the end of the year.

It is important to budget for the payment of taxes that may be due on your alimony. Taxes are also another item to consider when looking at your monthly living expenses for the purposes of seeking an alimony award.

Make sure to discuss the specifics with your attorney and your tax advisor. Both spouses should treat the alimony as deductible and taxable or both should not. If the IRS sees that one spouse does, and one does not, somebody is going to get audited or receive that Notice of Taxes Due.

14.6   During the divorce proceedings, is our tax filing status affected?

It can be. You are considered unmarried if your decree is final by December 31 of the tax year. Under Georgia law, your decree becomes final the day it is entered by the court. However, be aware that there is always time to file an appeal, which is thirty days in Georgia.

If you are considered unmarried, your filing status is either "single" or, under certain circumstances, "head of household." If your decree is not final as of December 31, your filing status is either "married filing a joint return" with you both cooperating, or "married filing a separate return," unless you live apart from your spouse and meet the exception for "head of household."

While your divorce is in progress, talk to both your tax advisor and your attorney about your filing status. It may be beneficial to figure your tax on both a joint return and a separate return to see which gives you the lower tax. IRS Publication 504, Divorced or Separated Individuals, provides more detail on tax issues while you are going through a divorce.

14.7 Should I file a joint income tax return with my spouse while our divorce is pending?

Consult your tax advisor to determine the risks and benefits of filing a joint return with your spouse. Compare this with the consequences of filing your tax return separately. Sometimes the overall tax liability will be less with the filing of a joint return, but other factors are important to consider.

When deciding whether to file a joint return with your spouse, consider any concerns you have about the accuracy and truthfulness of the information on the tax return. If you have any doubts, consult both your attorney and your tax advisor before agreeing to sign a joint tax return with your spouse. Prior to filing a return with your spouse, try to reach agreement, or expect a dispute later, about how any tax owed or refund expected will be shared, and ask your lawyer to assist you in getting this in writing.

14.8 For tax purposes, is one time of year better to divorce than another?

It depends upon your tax situation. If you and your spouse agree that it would be beneficial to file joint tax returns for the year in which you are divorcing, you may wish to not have your divorce finalized before the end of the year.

Your marital status for filing income taxes is determined by your status on December 31. Consequently, if you both want to preserve your right to file a joint return, your decree should not be entered before December 31 of that year.

14.9 What tax consequences should I consider regarding the sale of our home?

When your home is sold, whether during your divorce or after, the sale may be subject to a capital gains tax. If your home was your primary residence and you lived in the home for two of the preceding five years, you may be eligible to exclude up to $250,000 of the gain on the sale of your home. If both you and your spouse meet the ownership and residence tests, you may be eligible to exclude up to $500,000 of the gain.

If you anticipate the gain on the sale of your residence to be more than $250,000, talk with your attorney and your tax advisor early in the divorce process about a plan to minimize the tax liability. For more information, see IRS Publication 523, Selling Your Home, or visit the IRS website at www.irs.gov and talk with your tax advisor. These capital gains laws change, so confirm the existing law in your case.

14.10 How might capital gains tax be a problem for me years after the divorce?

Future capital gains tax on the sale of property should be discussed with your attorney and your tax advisor during the negotiation and trial preparation stages of your case. This is especially important if the sale of the property is imminent. Failure to do so may result in an unfair outcome.

For example, suppose you agree that your spouse will be awarded the proceeds from the sale of your home valued at $200,000, after the real estate commission, and you will take the stock portfolio also valued at $200,000.

Suppose that, after the divorce, you decide to sell the stock. It is still valued at $200,000, but you learn that its original price was $120,000 and that you must pay capital gains tax of 15 percent on the $80,000 of gain. You pay tax of $12,000, leaving you with $188,000.

Meanwhile, your former spouse sells the marital home but pays no capital gains tax because it qualifies for the $250,000 exemption, leaving that spouse with the full $200,000.

Tax implications of your property division should always be discussed with your attorney and your tax advisor.

14.11 During and after the divorce, who gets to claim the children as dependents?

Many Georgia judges will not even address this issue in court. These judges usually defer to the IRS rules. The general IRS rule is that whoever the child lives with 51 percent of the time gets to claim the exemption for the child. There are exceptions, such as when the parents agree to split the exemption, and IRS Form 8332 is used.

If claiming your child is an important issue for you, then discuss this with your attorney and your financial advisor. It is helpful if you review the IRS guidelines (available at www.irs. gov) prior to any discussion. *See* IRS Publications 501 (Exemptions, Standard Deductions, and Filing Information) and 504 (Divorced or Separated Individuals).

14.12 My decree says I have to sign IRS Form 8332 so my former spouse can claim our child as an exemption, because I have custody. Should I sign it once for all future years?

No. IRS Publication 501 explains the specific rules regarding exemptions for dependents, including the forms that have to be provided and an explanation of what is required to revoke a release to claim an exemption.

Additionally, child custody and child support can be modified in the future. If there is a future modification of custody or support, which parent is entitled to claim your child as an exemption could change. The best practice is to provide your former spouse a timely copy of Form 8332 signed by you for the appropriate tax year only.

If the court ordered you to allow your former spouse to claim the child and you have custody, then you need to discuss this with your attorney and your tax advisor right away.

14.13 Can my spouse and I split the child-care tax credit for child-care expenses?

No. IRS Publication 503 addresses the child and dependent-care expenses. Any specific questions should be directed to your tax advisor.

According to the Georgia Child Support Guidelines, the value of the federal income tax credit for child care may be considered when determining the payor parent's obligation for child support.

The value of the federal child-care tax credit may be subtracted from the actual costs of child care to arrive at a figure for net child-care expenses owed by the parent paying support. Or the federal child tax credit may be subtracted from the final child-support amount. (If subtracting the credit from the child-support obligation, make sure to divide the credit by twelve months and subtract a portion of the credit monthly.)

Only the custodial parent is allowed to claim the credit. If you are a noncustodial parent and paying child care, talk to your lawyer about how to address this issue in your divorce decree.

14.14   Is the cost of getting a divorce, including my attorney fees, tax deductible under any circumstances?

Your legal fees for getting a divorce are not deductible. However, a portion of your attorney fees may be deductible if they are for these uses:

- The collection of sums included in your gross income, such as alimony or interest income
- Advice regarding the determination of taxes or tax due

Attorney fees are "miscellaneous" deductions for individuals and, under law current at the time of this publication, are consequently limited to 2 percent of your adjusted gross income. More details can be found in IRS Publication 529, Miscellaneous Deductions.

You may also be able to deduct fees you pay to appraisers or accountants who help you. Talk to your tax advisor about whether any portion of your attorney fees or other expenses from your divorce is deductible.

14.15   Do I have to complete a new form W-4 for my employer because of my divorce?

Completing a new form W-4, Employee's Withholding Certificate, will help you to claim the proper withholding allowances based upon your marital status and exemptions. Also, if you are receiving alimony, you may need to make quarterly estimated tax payments. Consult with your tax advisor to ensure you are making the most beneficial tax-planning decision.

14.16   What is *innocent spouse relief* and how can it help me?

Innocent spouse relief refers to a method of obtaining relief from the Internal Revenue Service for taxes owed as a result of a joint income tax return filed during your marriage. An example is when your spouse without your knowledge hid taxable income or falsely claimed expenses on Form 1040-Schedule C (Profit or Loss from a Business) for a business in which you had no responsibility. Numerous factors affect your eligibility for innocent spouse tax relief, such as:

- You would suffer a financial hardship if you were required to pay the tax.
- You did not significantly benefit from the unpaid taxes.
- You suffered abuse during your marriage.
- You thought your spouse would pay the taxes on the original return.

Talk with your attorney and your tax advisor if you are concerned about liability for taxes arising from joint tax returns filed during the marriage. You may benefit from a referral to an attorney who specializes in tax law.

15

Military Divorce

*Military service while married deserves, for that alone,
a medal to both spouses who serve faithfully.*

At any given time there are approximately 1.3 million people on active duty in the U.S. military and another 850,000 people in the reserves. These numbers do not include the countless millions of retired military. The successful military marriage requires tough independence by both spouses during deployments and patient readjustment by both when deployment ends. Unfortunately, the divorce rate for these service members is higher than for many other professions.

As with many divorces, issues with the children and issues with money may be the biggest problems. However, military families usually find these problems to be more pronounced because of the frequent absence of the military parent and the unwillingness or inability of the spouse staying at home to live like a single parent. The need for both parents to readjust upon the military parent's return adds further stress because both parents have changed to some degree in order to survive the separation or their environment.

The military lifestyle of frequent moves, deployments, and high-stress situations causes marital problems to be amplified. It is because of these concerns that it is important to consult with a lawyer who understands your situation and can help you navigate the difficult terrain.

15.1 What is a *military divorce?*

A *military divorce* is the term used for a divorce when at least one party is or was employed by the U.S. military. Divorces are governed by state law and each state has its own set of laws governing divorces. The federal government does not have any direct laws regarding divorces. However, when a party to a divorce is in the military, there are certain aspects of the case that are governed by that party's employment with the U.S. military.

If you or your spouse are or were in the military, then it is important for you to speak with a family law attorney who has experience handling military divorces in Georgia.

15.2 My spouse is in the military. What are my rights to benefits after the divorce?

As the former spouse of a military member, the types of benefits to which you may be entitled are typically determined by the number of years you were married, the number of years your spouse was in the military while you were married, and whether or not you have remarried. Be sure you obtain accurate information about these dates.

You may be eligible for:

- A portion of your spouse's military retirement pay
- A survivor benefit in the event of your spouse's death
- Health care or participation in a temporary, transitional health-care program
- Use of certain military facilities, such as the commissary

While your divorce is pending, educate yourself about your right to future military benefits so that you can plan for your future with clarity. If your divorce is still pending, contact your base legal office, or, for more information, visit the website for the branch of the military in which your spouse is or was a member.

15.3 What special rules are there for a service member's divorce in Georgia? What is the *ten-year rule*?

According to federal law *(Uniformed Services Former Spouses' Protection Act 10 U.S. Code 1408)*, to be eligible for direct payment to a spouse by the *Defense Finance and Accounting Service (DFAS)* of a property division of military retired pay, the spouse must be married to that service member for at least ten years, and at least ten years of the marriage must also be during the spouse's military active duty service.

It is important to remember that the so-called ten-year rule is a federal rule, not a Georgia rule. *The Uniformed Services Former Spouses' Protection Act* makes it clear the court in a state (not federal laws) decodes how and what marital property is divided between the parties, including military retired pay. The ten-year rule prohibits the DFAS only from issuing payment directly to the spouse of military retired pay that is awarded by the court as a property division with a marriage not meeting the ten-year rule. It does not prohibit a state court from dividing military retired pay as a property division.

So, if a court divides retired pay as a property division between parties married only nine years, DFAS will not pay it out to the dependent spouse. In that event, the amount awarded could be collected by other means, such as by garnishment of the service member's personal bank account.

It is important to note that the ten-year rule does not apply to alimony payments. So, if the military retired pay is being divided or awarded under the provisions for alimony, then DFAS will pay such alimony award to the spouse even if married less than ten years.

15.4 My spouse is stationed in Texas, but I live in Georgia with our children. Where do we file the divorce?

Because divorce is governed by state law, you would look to the law of the state that you permanently reside in (the legal word is *domicile*). If you and the children live in Georgia and the only reason that your spouse is in Texas is because of military orders, then the divorce may be filed in Georgia.

However, if neither of you were previously a *bona fide* or domiciliary resident of Georgia, you have to make sure that you meet Georgia's six-month residency requirement for the court to have jurisdiction for your divorce action. Then you need to discuss with your attorney the specifics about giving your spouse proper notice of the divorce and making sure your spouse is served properly with the complaint.

15.5 I am stationed in Georgia. My spouse moved to Georgia with me, but we are originally from Michigan. Where do we file for divorce?

The general rule is that you should file for divorce in the state where you are domiciled, but that may be impracticable. In order to file for divorce in Georgia, you have to either be domiciled (a *bona fide* resident, meaning you live here now or have previously lived here, and while here have established "residency" with an intent to remain or return to Georgia if away) in Georgia for six months or more. You can file for divorce in Georgia without being a *bona fide* domiciliary resident (and thereby not losing status as a resident of another state where there may be no state income tax) if the military member has been currently stationed in Georgia for the past twelve months or more.

15.6 My spouse is stationed in Germany, but the children and I live in Georgia. Can my spouse file for divorce in Germany?

The general answer is that you have to file for divorce where you lived as a married couple to obtain personal jurisdiction of both spouses. If you don't have any connections with Germany, then the divorce is probably not proper there. If this is your situation, then you should contact an attorney immediately and discuss the specifics of military divorces when one spouse is overseas.

15.7 We are from California and we moved to Texas right after we got married because of my spouse's military orders and now we live in Georgia. Can we get divorced in Georgia?

Yes, if you meet the legal requirements. The answer is going to depend on the time frame in which you lived in each place. It is possible that two or three states may actually be able to handle your divorce, but the goal is to try to file in the best place to avoid any arguments over jurisdiction.

If you have been domiciled in Georgia for six months or more or if you are military and have been stationed in Georgia for twelve months or more, then you can file for divorce in Georgia.

Military divorces are very complicated and it is very difficult to determine the proper state in which to file the divorce. This is why it is very important for you to discuss these specifics with your attorney.

15.8 My spouse is in the military and refuses to give me any money. What can I do?

The best answer is to hire a lawyer and go to court and try to get the judge to issue an order giving you some temporary support. However, the other option would be to contact your spouse's chain of command or the inspector general (IG) where your spouse is stationed. Every branch of service has its own regulations regarding a service member supporting his or her dependents. Service members get paid extra when they have dependents and these regulations provide for a default amount of support if there is no agreement or order in place.

15.9 If my spouse is deployed, can I still file for divorce?

Yes. But the issue is going to be how much of the action can you proceed with while your spouse is deployed. If the military spouse consents and wants the divorce, then it's not a problem. If the military spouse does not consent to the divorce, then there will be a delay.

The court is very limited in what exactly it can or will order when a service member is deployed. Oftentimes the service member will invoke his or her rights under the *Servicemembers Civil Relief Act* and attempt to stop the proceedings until they are available from deployment.

This is another important reason why you should hire an attorney who has experience with divorces involving deployed spouses.

15.10 My spouse lives on a military installation. What is the process to serve the divorce papers on my military spouse?

Discuss this with your attorney. You should be able to contact your local sheriff or local process server and he or she should be able to get the service member served. There are special requirements, but the military installation is usually helpful in these matters, but are not required on a federal exclusive jurisdiction installation, to order the military member to voluntarily accept service of process.

15.11 What is *DFAS*?

Defense Finance and Accounting Service (DFAS) pays all Department of Defense (DoD) military and civilian personnel, retirees, and annuitants (recipients of a recurring payments, such as spousal share of military retirement), as well as major DoD contractors and vendors. For more information go to www.dfas.mil.

15.12 What about military retirement?

Discussing the division of military retirement could take up a few chapters if not the whole book. This is just a general overview. You need a lawyer who has divided it before. It's complicated and DFAS requires certain things to be addressed. In fact, if the wording of the order is not correct, then DFAS will disregard the order and not pay the money directly to the spouse and will consider the order invalid.

When discussing military retired pay you have to understand state and federal law and how the two coexist. Under federal law, military retired pay is allowed to be divided, but it is not required (the Supreme Court once held that under the federal law then existing, military retire pay was not divisible, but Congress enacted laws to change that ruling to now allow it).

Under Georgia law, military retired pay is an asset of the marriage and is subject to equitable division (to the extent that it was acquired during the marriage). Therefore, in Georgia a spouse could be married twenty years and get 0 percent of the retirement, or be married ten years and get 100 percent. Although neither of these situations is likely, they are possible.

Usually, a formula is used to divide military retired pay in Georgia. The formula is generally years of the marriage divided by years of service divided by two equals the percentage the spouse should receive.

15.13   What is the *ten-year rule*?

According to federal law *(Uniformed Services Former Spouses' Protection Act 10 U.S. Code 1408),* a spouse must be married to a service member for ten years overlapping ten years of military service of the member before DFAS may lawfully pay directly from the member's net disposable retirement pay to the spouse as an award of division of property by the court.

It is important to remember that Georgia does not have a ten-year rule and the issue that arises between these two laws in Georgia is just the payment of military retired pay as a division of retired pay, but does not apply to an award of alimony.

15.14   Will I be able to collect child support from my military spouse?

Each branch of service has its own regulations regarding service members supporting their dependents. This is an important thing to remember if court is not available. Sometimes the formula in these regulations works out to equal Georgia child support and other times it doesn't. Georgia uses child-support worksheets that factor in both parents' gross income as well as the child's needs.

Georgia has a specific statute regarding gross income of a service member and it says to include: base pay, *basic allowance for subsistence (BAS),* and *basic allowance for housing (BAH)* at the nonlocale without dependents rate—but whether to include special incentive pay or not is in the judge's discretion.

15.15   What is the *Servicemembers Civil Relief Act?*

To quote the U.S. Department of Justice Civil Rights Division (www.justice.gov/crt/about/hce/documents/scra_qa_5-26-11.pdf): *"The Servicemembers Civil Relief Act (SCRA),* formerly known as the *Soldiers' and Sailors' Civil Relief Act (SS-CRA),* is a federal law that provides protections to individuals in military service. The law's purpose is to postpone, suspend, terminate, or reduce the amount of certain civil obligations so that members of the armed forces and certain other individuals can focus their full attention on their military or professional responsibilities without adverse consequences for themselves or their families."

For more information go to the American Bar Association's website: www.americanbar.org/portals/public_resources/aba_home_front/information_center/servicemembers_civil_relief_act.html.

If you believe that the SCRA is applicable to your case, then discuss the matter with your attorney.

15.16   What is an *LES*?

LES stands for *Leave and Earnings Statement* and in the simplest of terms it is a pay stub for a government employee. "The LES is a comprehensive statement of a member's leave and earnings showing their entitlements, deductions, allotments (fields not used for Reserve and National Guard members), leave information, tax withholding information, and Thrift Savings Plan (TSP) information" (www.dfas.mil/militarymembers.html).

A service member can acesss military pay records twenty-four hours a day on myPay—an online portal. (https://mypay.dfas.mil/mypay.aspx) For a more detailed description and how to understand an LES, you can visit DFAS at www.dfas.mil/militarymembers.html and scroll down to the section labeled "Understanding Your LES."

15.17   My spouse is on active duty and we are getting a divorce. Can I still be covered under TRICARE?

Maybe. If you have been married for at least twenty years and your spouse served on active duty for at least twenty years, and the marriage overlapped the service for at least twenty years then you can continue to receive TRICARE benefits. (TRICARE is the health-care program for service members.) If you have been married for less than twenty years then the general answer is "no," but there are special rules that apply that could change the answer to "yes."

If you are in this situation, then it is best to have an attorney who is familiar with military benefits and divorces and understands what options are available to you. For more general information go to www.tricare.mil/.

15.18 Does Georgia have any special requirements regarding parenting time before, during, or after a deployment?

Yes. Georgia law allows the court to enter a temporary modification order for the parenting plan to ensure contact with the child during the period of deployment. The law also says that the court should hear matters affecting parenting time because of deployments as soon as possible and they shall be a priority on the court's calendar.

This Georgia law also allows the court to order the following:

- The nondeploying parent to make the child reasonably available to the deploying parent to exercise parenting time immediately before and after the deploying parent departs for deployment and whenever the deploying parent returns to or from leave or furlough from deployment

- The nondeploying parent to facilitate opportunities for the deployed parent to have regular and continuing contact with the child by telephone, e-mail exchanges, virtual video parenting time through the Internet, or any other similar means

- The nondeploying parent to not interfere with the delivery of correspondence or packages between the deployed parent and child

- The deploying parent to provide timely information regarding military leave and departure schedule to the nondeploying parent

Because actual leave from a deployment and departure dates for a deployment are subject to change with little notice due to military necessity, such changes shall not be used by the nondeploying parent to prevent contact between the deployed parent and the child.

15.19 With our military status, will the military legal assistance office represent us in the divorce process?

Depending on local availability, some military installation legal offices will, as a minimum, provide counselling and basic advice. Others might prepare a standard-type settlement agreement. Unless that legal officer is a member of the Georgia Bar, caution warrants the proposed agreement being reviewed by a Georgia attorney to ensure it complies with the standards a Georgia judge will approve. Of course, due to conflict-of-interest rules, one legal office can represent only one spouse, not both. Very few legal offices will prepare the divorce complaint or other pleadings, and fewer yet are authorized to appear in civilian court. There is an approved program called *Legal Assistance for Military Personnel (LAMP),* that under certain circumstances allows representation of military members. The Georgia State Bar link is: www.gabar.org/PublicService/ MilitaryLegalAssistance.cfm. Georgia Legal Services provides representation and attorney referrals for low-income parties. Visit: www.glsp.org.

16

Going to Court

No one has ever loved anyone the way
everyone wants to be loved.
–Ms. Mignon McLaughlin

For many of us, our images of going to court are created by movie scenes and our favorite television shows. We picture the witness breaking down in tears after a grueling cross-examination. We see lawyers strutting around the courtroom, waving their arms as they plead their case to the jury.

Hollywood drama, however, is a far cry from reality. Going to court for your divorce can mean many things, ranging from sitting in a hallway while waiting for the lawyers and judges to conclude a conference, to being on the witness stand giving mundane answers to questions about your monthly living expenses.

Regardless of the nature of your court proceeding, going to court often evokes a sense of anxiety. Perhaps your divorce might be the first time in your life that you have even been in a courtroom. Be assured that these feelings of nervousness and uncertainty are normal.

Understanding what will occur in court and being well prepared for any court hearings will relieve much of your stress. Knowing the order of events, courtroom etiquette, the role of the people in the courtroom, and what is expected of you will make the entire experience easier.

Your lawyer will be with you at all times to support you any time you go to court. Remember, every court appearance moves you one step closer to completing your divorce so that you can move forward with your life.

16.1 What do I need to know about appearing in court and court dates in general?

Court dates are important. As soon as you receive a notice from your lawyer about a court date in your case, confirm whether your attendance will be required and put it on your calendar.

Ask your lawyer about the nature of the hearing, including whether the judge will be listening to testimony by witnesses, reading affidavits, or merely listening to the arguments of the lawyers.

Ask whether it is necessary for you to meet with your lawyer or take any other action to prepare for the hearing, such as providing additional information or documents.

Find out how long the hearing is expected to last. It may be as short as a few minutes or as long as a day or more.

If you plan to attend the hearing, determine where and when to meet your lawyer. Depending upon the type of hearing, your lawyer may want you to arrive in advance of the scheduled hearing time to prepare.

Make sure you know the location of the courthouse, where to park, and the floor and room number of the courtroom. Planning for such simple matters as having change available for a parking meter can eliminate unnecessary stress. If you want someone to go to court with you to provide you support, check with your lawyer first.

16.2 When and how often will I need to go to court?

When and how often you will need to go to court depends upon a number of factors. Depending upon the complexity of your case, you may have only one hearing or numerous court hearings throughout the course of your divorce.

Some hearings, usually those on procedural matters, are attended only by the attorneys. These could include requests for the other side to provide information or for the setting of certain deadlines. These hearings are often brief and held in the judge's chambers rather than in the courtroom (these hearings are often referred to as a *status conference* or a *pretrial conference*). Other hearings, such as temporary hearings (*see* question 16.8) or support, are typically attended by both parties and their attorneys.

If you and your spouse settle all of the issues in your case, a final "uncontested" hearing may be held (*see* question 16.10). If your case proceeds to a contested trial, your appearance will be required for the duration of the trial. In Georgia, divorce matters can be heard by a judge or a jury (but only the judge can decide issues of custody and visitation. Either party can request a jury trial.

16.3 How much notice will I get about the need to appear in court?

The amount of notice you will get for any court hearing can vary from a few days to several weeks. Ask your attorney when it will be necessary for you to appear in court on your case so that you can have ease in preparing and planning.

If you receive a notice of a hearing, immediately contact your attorney, who can tell you whether your appearance is required and what other steps are needed to prepare.

16.4 I am afraid to be alone in the same room with my spouse. When I go to court, is this going to happen if the attorneys go into the judge's office to discuss the case?

Talk to your lawyer. Prior to any court hearing, you and your spouse may be asked to wait while your attorneys meet with the judge to discuss preliminary matters.

A number of options are likely to be available to ensure that you feel safe. These might include having you or your spouse wait in different locations or having a friend or family member present. If these meetings take place in the courthouse, then there will most likely be a bailiff available to keep the parties separated.

Your attorney wants to support you in feeling secure throughout all court proceedings. Just let your attorney know of your concerns.

16.5 Do I have to go to court every time there is a court hearing on any motion?

Not necessarily. Some matters will be decided by the judge after listening to the arguments of the attorneys. These hearings are usually held in the judge's office, referred to as *chambers,* and you will not be required to attend. Any time there is a hearing or a motion before the judge, you should discuss it with your lawyer and find out if your attendance is required or not.

16.6 My spouse's attorney keeps asking for *continuances* of court dates. Is there anything I can do to stop this?

Continuances of court dates are not unusual in divorces. A court date might be postponed for many reasons, including a conflict on the calendar of one of the attorneys or the judge, the lack of availability of one of the parties or an important witness, or the need for more time to prepare.

Discuss with your attorney your desire to move your case forward without further delay, if that is what you truly want, so that repeated requests for continuances can be vigorously resisted. Sometimes a necessary delay can benefit a spouse who needs to hold onto medical health insurance a while longer, or for other reasons, when a final divorce decree will cause hardship that is better delayed.

16.7 If I have to go to court, will I be put on the stand? Will there be a jury?

It's possible you may need to offer evidence that only you can provide, and that is done by your testimony. In Georgia, either party can request that the divorce be heard by a jury; however, only the judge can decide issues of custody and visitation of the children. Whether you will be put on the stand will depend upon the nature of the issues in dispute, the judge assigned to your case, and your attorney's strategy for your case. More than likely you will be called to testify at some point in your case—after all, it is your case and the judge or the jury needs to hear your side.

16.8   My attorney said I need to be in court for our *tempo-rary hearing* next week. What's going to happen?

A *temporary hearing* is held to determine the rights of the parties on a temporary basis. The judge will usually decide matters such as who remains in the house while your divorce is pending, which parent the children are going to live with, the setting up of a visitation schedule, and who is going to pay which bills (this includes a decision on temporary child support and spousal support, if any).

You should always plan to attend your temporary hearing. Most temporary hearings occur in the courtroom and are like a mini-trial. At temporary hearings the parties involved and one additional witness for each side may give oral testimony. Any additional witnesses must testify by deposition or affidavit unless otherwise ordered by the court. Generally, you can present as many affidavits on your behalf as you want (it is important to know that there are certain requirements that have to be met for affidavits to be admissible).

The procedure for your temporary hearing can vary depending upon the county in which your case was filed, the judge to which the case is assigned, and whether temporary custody is disputed. In some counties, your hearing will be one of many on that day's court docket. You may find yourself in a courtroom with many other lawyers and their clients, all having matters scheduled before the court that day. You should be present or available because your attorney may need additional information from you during the hearing, and last-minute negotiations to resolve temporary issues are not uncommon.

If temporary custody is disputed, you and other witnesses might be required to take the witness stand to give testimony at your temporary hearing.

It is important to discuss your case with your attorney in advance. Ask him or her about the procedure you should expect for the temporary hearing in your case.

16.9   Will the judge talk to my children?

Generally, minor children are not allowed to testify and they are usually excluded from the courtroom. However, if custody is in dispute, then a party can request, or the judge can order, that the judge have a "consultation" with the children.

This consultation is within the judge's discretion, and the attorneys for the parties can be present, but generally can't question the child. This consultation can be recorded if it is requested in advance.

16.10 Do I have to go to court if all of the issues in my case are settled?

Under Georgia law, a final court hearing may be held even if you and your spouse have settled your case. In most cases only the plaintiff (the spouse who filed the divorce complaint) will be required to attend.

If you are the plaintiff, plan to attend a final hearing for your divorce. If you are the defendant—the spouse who did not file the complaint—ask your attorney whether you must or should attend the final hearing.

These hearings are referred to as *uncontested* hearings and are usually short. At an uncontested hearing one of the parties "proves" his or her case to the judge by testifying to the basic facts of the marriage (simple facts you already know, such as: names and residency status of the parties, date of marriage, date of separation, status of the marriage being irretrievably broken, request that divorce be granted, and outline of the terms of the settlement or simply identification of the signed agreement between the parties and asking for it to be approved and included in the final decree of divorce). You will not need to memorize all this information because your lawyer will have gathered all the facts from you earlier and will just ask you to confirm these matters.

16.11 Are there any rules about courtroom etiquette that I need to know?

Knowing a few tips about being in the courtroom will make your experience easier.

- Dress appropriately. Avoid overly casual dress, lots of jewelry, revealing clothing, and extreme hairstyles.
- Don't bring beverages into the courtroom. Most courts have rules that do not allow food and drink in courtrooms. If you need water, ask your attorney.
- Dispose of chewing gum before entering the courtroom.

- Don't talk aloud in the courtroom unless you're on the witness stand or being questioned by the judge.
- Do not enter the judge's office.
- Stand up whenever the judge is entering or leaving the courtroom.
- Be sure to turn off your cell phone or silence any other electronic devices to avoid confiscation by the bailiff if your device disturbs the court.

Although you may feel anxious initially, you'll likely feel more relaxed about the courtroom setting once your hearing gets underway.

16.12   What is the role of the *bailiff?*

The *bailiff's* main job is to provide security to the judge. Bailiffs also provides support for the judge and attorneys in the management of the courtroom. Along with protecting the judge, bailiffs are tasked with maintaining order in the courtroom.

16.13   Will there be a *court reporter,* and what does the reporter do?

A *court reporter* is a professional trained to make an accurate record of the words spoken and documents offered into evidence during court proceedings. Some counties use tape-recording devices rather than court reporters.

A written transcript of a court proceeding may be purchased from the court reporter. If your case is appealed, the transcript prepared by the court reporter will be used by the appeals court to review the evidence and proceedings in your case.

The court reporter often is seated near a clerk of the court, who is responsible for maintaining the court's case file and securing documents and other items offered into evidence at trial.

Some hearings or colloquies/discussions are held "off the record," which means that the court reporter is not making a record of what is being said. Ordinarily, these are matters for which no appeal is expected to be taken.

Some courts do not routinely have court reporters present for a case unless expressly requested. Therefore, it is always better to confirm with your attorney whether you want a court reporter to record the proceedings, and if so, whether the reporter must be requested in advance and whether to make arrangements to have a reporter present rather than rely on the other party or the court to do so.

16.14 Will I be able to talk to my attorney while we are in court?

During court proceedings it is important that your attorney give full attention to anything being said by the judge, witnesses, or your spouse's attorney. For this reason, your attorney will avoid talking with you when anyone else in the courtroom is speaking.

Plan to have pen and paper with you when you go to court. If your court proceeding is underway and your attorney is listening to what is being said by others in the courtroom, write a note with your questions or comments for your attorney to consider.

It is critical that your attorney hear each question asked by the other attorney and all answers given by each witness. If not, opportunities for making objections to inappropriate evidence may be lost. You can support your attorney in doing an effective job for you by avoiding talking while a court hearing is in progress.

If your court hearing is lengthy, breaks will be taken. You can use this time to discuss with your attorney any questions or observations you have about the proceeding.

16.15 What questions might my attorney ask me at the final hearing about the problems in our marriage and why I want the divorce?

Because Georgia is a no-fault state, your lawyer will usually ask you questions to show the court that the marriage is irretrievably broken, without going into detail about the specific difficulties in your marriage. Although the grounds of adultery and mental cruelty are still on the books, they are usually not pursued, unless it fits a sound strategy not otherwise attainable.

The questions will be similar to these:

Attorney: "You and your spouse separated on _____ date?"

You: "Yes."

Attorney: "Since that date you and your spouse have lived in a *bona fide* state of separation?"

You: "Yes."

Attorney: "You are here asking the court to grant you a divorce because your marriage is irretrievably broken?"

You: "Yes."

Attorney: "Is your marriage irretrievably broken?"

You: "Yes."

Attorney: "Is there any reasonable prospect of reconciliation?"

You: "No."

A spouse who disagrees may give an opposite opinion that the marriage can be saved. However, most judges recognize that it takes two willing partners for a marriage to be reconciled. So long as one spouse says the marriage is over, it is over. Agreement is not necessary.

It is unlikely that you will be asked in great detail about the nature of the marital problems that led to the divorce. In the majority of cases, questions like those above will satisfy the judge that the requirements under Georgia law for the dissolving of a marriage have been met.

16.16 My attorney said that the judge has issued a *pretrial order* having to do with my upcoming trial and that we'll have to comply with it. What does this mean?

A *pretrial order* is basically a script for how you want the trial to go. It is a layout so the judge can follow along with what evidence you anticipate putting forward.

Ask your lawyer for a copy of the pretrial order. Some judges will order that certain information be provided either to the opposing party or to the judge in advance of trial. This might include:

- A list of issues that have been settled
- A list of issues that are still disputed
- Agreements, referred to as *stipulations,* as to the truth of certain facts

- The names of witnesses
- Exhibits
- A summary of how you want the judge to decide the case

Deadlines are given for providing the information.

16.17 What is a *pretrial conference*?

A *pretrial conference* is a meeting held with the attorneys and the judge to review information related to an upcoming trial, such as how long the trial is expected to last, the issues in dispute, and the law surrounding the disputed issues. Often the trial date is set at the pretrial conference.

If a pretrial conference is held in your case, ask your attorney whether you should attend. Your attorney may request that you either be present for the conference or be available by phone.

16.18 Besides meeting with my attorney, is there anything else I should do to prepare for my upcoming trial?

Yes. Be sure to review your deposition and any information you provided in your discovery, such as answers to interrogatories. It is also important to go back and review any important documents (bank records, pay stubs, tax information, for example). At trial, it is possible that you will be asked some of the same questions that you have previously been asked and it's possible that you will be questioned on certain documents. If you think you might give different answers at trial, discuss this with your attorney.

It is important that your attorney know in advance of trial whether any information you provided during the discovery process has changed.

16.19 I'm meeting with my attorney to prepare for trial. How do I make the most of these meetings?

Meeting with your attorney to prepare for your trial is important to achieving a good outcome. Before the meeting, you should reread all the important documents in your case and come to the meeting prepared to discuss the following:

- The issues in your case
- Your desired outcome on each of the issues

- The questions you might be asked at trial by both attorneys
- The exhibits that will be offered into evidence during the trial
- The witnesses for your trial
- The status of negotiations

Your meeting with your attorney will help you better understand what to expect at your trial and make the trial experience easier. Additionally, the better prepared you are, the better the meeting will go, allowing you and your lawyer to focus on the important issues.

16.20 My attorney says that the law firm is busy with *trial preparation*. What exactly is my attorney doing to prepare for my trial?

Countless tasks are necessary and have to be performed to adequately prepare your case for trial. These are just some of them:

- Developing arguments to be made on each of the contested issues
- Researching and reviewing the relevant law in your case
- Reviewing the facts of your case to determine which witnesses are best suited to testifying about them
- Reviewing, selecting, and preparing exhibits
- Preparing questions for all witnesses
- Preparing an opening statement
- Reviewing rules on evidence to prepare for any objections to be made or opposed at trial
- Determining the order of witnesses and all exhibits
- Reviewing any adverse evidence the other side plans on using
- Preparing your file for the day of court, including preparing a trial notebook with essential information

Your attorney is committed to a good outcome for you in your divorce and will be engaged in many important actions to fully prepare your case for trial.

16.21 My divorce is scheduled for trial. Does this mean there is no hope for a settlement?

Many cases are settled after a trial date is set. Some cases even settle on the night before or the day of trial, hence the saying "My case settled on the eve of trial."

The setting of a trial date may cause you and your spouse to think about the risks and costs of going to trial. This can help you and your spouse focus on what is most important to you and lead you toward a negotiated settlement. Because the costs of preparing for and proceeding to trial are substantial, it is best to engage in settlement negotiations well in advance of your trial date. If a settlement is important to you then discuss this with your lawyer and make sure your desires are clearly known.

16.22 Can I prevent my spouse from being in the courtroom?

No. Because your spouse has a legal interest in the outcome of your divorce, he or she has the right to be present. Georgia courtrooms are also open to the public, and it is not uncommon even for persons uninvolved in your divorce to pass through the courtroom at various times simply because they have other business with the court.

16.23 Can I take a friend or family member with me to court?

Yes. Let your attorney know in advance if you intend to bring anyone to court with you. Some people important to you may be very emotional about your divorce or your spouse. Be sure to invite someone who is better able to focus attention on supporting you rather than on their own feelings. Do not bring a new intimate friend to court—that is a recipe for disaster.

16.24 Can my friends and family be present in the courtroom during my trial?

It depends upon whether they will be witnesses in your case. In most cases where witnesses other than the husband and wife are testifying, the attorneys request that the court "sequester" the witnesses. The judge would then order all witnesses, except you and your spouse, to leave the courtroom until after they have testified.

A witness who has completed testifying and has been "permanently excused" from the subpoena will ordinarily be allowed to remain in the courtroom for the remainder of the trial.

If the person is not testifying in your case then, he or she will be allowed to remain in the courtroom.

16.25   I want to do a great job testifying as a witness in my divorce trial. What are some tips?

Keep the following in mind to be a good witness on your own behalf:

- Tell the truth. Although this may not always be comfortable, it is critical if you want any or all of your testimony to be believed by the judge.

- Listen carefully to the complete question before thinking of your answer. Wait to consider your answer until after the full question is asked.

- Slow down. It's natural to speed up our speech when we are anxious. Taking your time with your answers ensures that the judge hears you and that the court reporter can accurately record your testimony.

- If you don't understand a question or don't know the answer, be sure to say so.

- If the question calls for a "yes" or "no" answer, simply say so. Then wait for the attorney to ask you the next question. If there is more you want to explain, remember that you have already told your attorney all of the important facts and he or she will make sure you are allowed to give any testimony significant in your case.

- Don't argue with the judge or the lawyers.

- Take your time. You may be asked some questions that call for a thoughtful response. If you need a moment to reflect on an answer before you give it, allow yourself that time.

- Stop speaking if an objection is made by one of the attorneys. Wait until the judge has decided whether to allow you to answer. "Overruled" means you may continue testifying as if no objection had been made.

209

"Sustained" means you say no more until the lawyer asks you another question.

16.26 Should I be worried about being cross-examined by my spouse's attorney at trial?

If your case goes to trial, prepare to be asked some questions by your spouse's attorney. Many of these questions will call for a simple "yes" or "no." Remember, answer the questions and then explain your answers, but only explain when essential. Not every answer needs explaining.

If you are worried about particular questions, discuss your concerns with your attorney, who can support you in giving a truthful response. Focus on preparing well for being asked questions by your spouse's attorney. Try not to take the questions personally; remember that the attorney is fulfilling a duty to advocate for your spouse's interest. Remember that you are just doing your best to tell the truth about the facts.

The best way to prepare for cross-examination is to think back on all the issues that your spouse has raised since right before the divorce, and then try to imagine the questions that your spouse's lawyer would ask regarding those issues.

16.27 What happens on the day of trial?

Although no two trials are alike, the following steps will occur in most divorce trials:

- Attorneys discuss procedural issues with the judge, such as how many witnesses will be called, how long the case will take to present, and when breaks might be taken.
- Attorneys give opening statements.
- Plaintiff's attorney calls plaintiff's witnesses to testify. Defendant's attorney may cross-examine each of them.
- Defendant's attorney calls defendant's witnesses to testify. Plaintiff's attorney may cross-examine each of them.
- Plaintiff's attorney calls any rebuttal witnesses, that is, witnesses whose testimony contradicts the testimony of the defendant's witnesses.
- Closing arguments are made first by plaintiff's attorney and then by defendant's attorney.

- If it's a jury trial, then the judge will read jury charges (or instructions on the law) to the jury.
- The jury will be sent to the deliberation room to deliberate and reach a decision in your case on all issues needed.

16.28 When a trial is without a jury, will the judge decide my case the day I go to court?

Sometimes. Often there is so much information presented in a judge-only (bench trial) case to consider that it is not possible for the judge to give an immediate ruling.

The judge may want to review documents, review the law, perform calculations, review trial notes, and give thoughtful consideration to the issues to be decided. For this reason, it may be days, weeks, or in some cases even longer before a ruling is made.

When a judge does not make a ruling immediately upon the conclusion of a trial, it is said that the case has been "taken under advisement."

16.29 Will the jury decide my case the day I go to court?

Yes, usually. The judge will give the jury instructions at the close of the trial. If a decision cannot be reached that day, the judge will bring the jury back the next day to continue their deliberations until they reach a decision. If the jury cannot reach a decision, then the judge could order that the case be retried with a different jury.

17

The Appeals Process

When an appeals court reverses a trial judge,
it does not necessarily mean the trial judge was wrong;
it just means that the appeals court comes later.

You may find that despite your best efforts to settle your case, your divorce went to trial and the judge (or jury) made major decisions that will have a serious impact on your future. It is the rare case that both parties are happy with the trial court's judgment. One or both of you may be either gravely disappointed or even shocked by the judgment.

The court might have seen your case differently than you and your attorney did. Perhaps the court made mistakes. It may be that the judge excluded under the rules of evidence (as interpreted by the trial judge) crucial evidence a party needed for a favorable outcome in his or her eyes, or it may be that Georgia law simply does not allow the outcome one of the parties wanted.

Whatever the reasons for the rulings, one of you may feel that the decisions are not ones that can be accepted without further effort. If this is the case, talk to your attorney immediately about your right to appeal. Together you can decide whether an appeal is in your best interest or whether it is better to accept the court's ruling and invest your energy in moving forward with your future.

17.1 How much time after my divorce do I have to file an appeal?

You must file an appeal within thirty days of the date the final order was filed by the clerk of the court. Because your attorney may also recommend filing certain motions following your trial, discuss your appeal rights with your attorney as soon as you have received the court's ruling.

A timely discussion with your attorney about your right to appeal is essential so important deadlines are not missed.

17.2 Can I appeal a temporary order?

Yes, but in limited circumstances. The rules regarding what type of appeal to pursue and which court to pursue the appeal before are very complex and are fact specific. It is important to discuss these issues with an attorney.

17.3 What parts of the decree can be appealed?

If you or your spouse are unhappy with final decisions made by the judge (or jury) in your case, either of you can file an appeal. Decisions that can be appealed include, but are not limited to: jurisdiction, custody, parenting time, child support, alimony, division of property, and attorney's fees.

17.4 Will my attorney recommend I appeal specific aspects of the decree, or will I have to request it?

Your attorney may advise you to file an appeal on certain issues of your case. You may also ask your attorney whether there is a legitimate basis for an appeal of any decision you believe is wrong. Talk to your attorney regarding the decisions most dissatisfying to you. Your attorney can advise which issues have the greatest likelihood of success on appeal, in light of the facts of your case and Georgia law.

17.5 When should an appeal be filed?

An appeal should be filed only after careful consultation with your attorney when you believe that the judge or jury has made a serious error under the law or the facts of your case. Among the factors you and your attorney should discuss are:

- Whether a motion for new trial is a preferred initial alternative
- Whether the judge or jury had authority under the law to make the decisions set forth in your decree
- The likelihood of the success of your appeal
- The risk that an appeal by you will encourage an appeal by your former spouse
- The cost of an appeal
- The length of time an appeal can be expected to take
- The impact of a delay in the case during the appeal

The deadline for filing an appeal is thirty days from the date that a final order is filed of record by the clerk of the court. It is important that you are clear about the deadline that applies in your case, so talk to your attorney at once if you are thinking about an appeal.

17.6   Are there any disadvantages to filing an appeal?

There can be disadvantages to filing an appeal, including:

- Uncertainty in the outcome
- Increased attorneys fees and costs
- The risk of a worse outcome on appeal than you received at trial
- Delay
- Prolonged conflict between you and your former spouse
- The risk of a second trial occurring after the appeal
- Difficulty in obtaining closure and moving forward with your life

17.7   Is an attorney necessary to appeal?

The appeals process is very detailed and specific, with set deadlines and specific court rules. Given the complex nature of the appellate process, you should have an attorney if you intend to file an appeal. Georgia family law cases are either heard by the Georgia Supreme Court or the Georgia Court of Appeals.

There are certain cases that can be directly appealed and there are other cases that have to be requested and approval obtained from the appellate courts (discretionary appeal). The right attorney can help you determine which court your case should be appealed to and what process has to be followed.

17.8 How long does the appeals process usually take?

It depends. An appeal can take anywhere from several months to well over a year. An appeal may also result in the appellate court requiring further proceedings by the trial court. This will result in further delay.

17.9 What are the steps in the appeals process?

There are many steps that your attorney will take on your behalf in the appeals process, including:

- Identifying the issues to be appealed
- Filing a notice with the court of your intent to appeal
- Obtaining the necessary court documents and trial exhibits to send to the appellate court
- Obtaining a transcript of the trial, a written copy of testimony by witnesses and statements by the judge and the lawyers made in the presence of the court reporter
- Performing legal research to support your arguments on appeal
- Preparing and filing a document known as a brief, which sets forth the facts of the case and the relevant law, complete with citations to court transcripts, court documents, and prior cases
- Making an oral argument before the judges of the appellate court

17.10 Is filing and pursuing an appeal expensive?

Yes. In addition to filing fees and attorney fees, there is likely to be a substantial cost for the preparation of the transcript of the trial testimony.

17.11 If I do not file an appeal, can I ever go back to court to change my decree?

Certain aspects of a decree are not modifiable, such as the division of property and debts or the award of attorney fees. Other parts of your decree, such as support or matters regarding the children, may be modified if there has been a "material and substantial change in circumstances."

A modification of custody or parenting time for minor children will also require you to show that the change would be in their best interest.

If your decree did not provide for alimony or if it ordered that the alimony be non-modifiable, it is unlikely that you will have any basis for a modification. If you believe that you have a basis for a modification of your divorce decree, consult with your attorney.

18

What Happens
after the Divorce?

*Upon issuance of the final decree of divorce, do not be
surprised to feel sadness at the end of your marriage, which
began with such great joy. A grieving period is normal.*

You have finally reached the end of your divorce journey. You may be feeling sad about the end of your
marriage, you may be feeling hopeful about the future, you
may be feeling scared about your new life coming to fruition,
or you may be feeling all of these things. These feelings are
normal. It is also normal for you to feel uneasy that your lawyer
is closing your file and you will be without the support to get
you through the days ahead. You may be feeling overwhelmed
and unsure about how you take the final actions to complete
property transfers or name-change details.

Whatever items are on your to-do list, it is best to map out
your action plan. Make sure you understand which items are
your responsibility and, as with everything through this divorce
process, start small.

18.1 What information must I give the court after my divorce?

Under Georgia law, you are not required to provide the
court with any additional information unless required to by the
court order. It is always helpful to make sure the court clerk
has a correct address on file for you in case something arises in
the future. Most court orders require parents to give each other
correct contact information when a minor child is involved.

18.2 What do I need to do when the amount of child support changes based on one of my children turning eighteen?

If you have more than one child, when one of your children reaches the age of majority (eighteen in Georgia), marries, dies, or becomes emancipated, the obligation amount of child support may be reduced pursuant to the terms of your decree. Sometimes your court order allows for this reduction to be automatic. This is why it is important to go back and review your order.

The payor's employer will need to be notified of the change so the child-support withdrawals from the payor's paycheck can be changed if it's being withheld automatically.

18.3 Do I need to inform the court if my employment changes?

If you pay support according to your decree and you change employers, it will be necessary for you to complete a new Notice to Withhold Income form for your new employer. You should do this as soon as possible to ensure child support is paid timely and to avoid an arrearage and interest charges.

18.4 My decree includes a provision that my former spouse and I both pay a portion of uninsured medical expenses, child-care expenses, or other expenses incurred for the minor children. How do I track this information and when do I get reimbursed?

Be sure to provide your former spouse with the appropriate documentation as set forth in your decree. Failure to request reimbursement of these expenses in a timely manner may result in your being barred from collecting them. Be sure to keep a copy of all documents you send to the other parent. Ensure claims are filed with health insurance companies within twelve months or the claim may be barred.

Reimbursement of uninsured medical expenses, as well as child-care or other related expenses, is an issue frequently disputed in modification and contempt of court matters. For this reason, maintain complete records regarding these expenses, such as:

- Copies of all billing statements from the service providers with your notations regarding payments made to include the date, amount, and check number
- Copies of all insurance benefits statements
- A monthly or an annual printout from your pharmacy of all the charges and payments for prescription drugs
- A monthly or annual printout from your child-care provider of all the charges and payments
- Copies of any correspondence between you and the other parent regarding these expenses
- A record of sums paid by the other parent, either directly to care providers or reimbursements paid to you

Keep these records organized by year and by child. You may want to consider creating a worksheet to help you track expenses and payments. In the event of a future dispute, you will then have all of the documentation needed for your attorney to present your case or to defend a claim against you.

18.5   What should I do if my former spouse and I have a disagreement about our parenting plan after the decree is entered?

Look to the terms of your agreement to find out what you need to do if there is a disagreement. A lot of newer agreements are providing that parties have to attend mediation before filing an action with the court.

If your former spouse does not cooperate with attendance at mediation or you are not required to attend mediation, document your request through a letter to your former spouse and schedule an appointment with an attorney to discuss your options, such as filing an action with the court to modify the decree.

18.6   How do I make my court-ordered payments that are not related to child support or alimony?

If have been ordered to pay an amount for property settlement, attorney fees, or guardian *ad litem* fees, you should review your court order to determine how and where to pay it. Keep proof of all payments made just in case—better safe than sorry!

18.7 My former spouse has not paid me the property settlement as ordered in the decree, what can I do?

In the event that your former spouse does not pay court-ordered judgments, enforcement mechanisms may be available, such as contempt of court actions or garnishment. If payment becomes a problem, contact your attorney to discuss your enforcement possibilities.

18.8 After my decree was entered, my former spouse did not pay a judgment and I did not do anything about it. Is it too late?

Judgments for property settlement or attorney fees will become dormant seven years after the date of the judgment (the date of your decree) or from the date of the last enforcement action. A *dormant judgment* is a judgment that is not enforced or executed within the required time frame. If your judgment becomes dormant, this means that the judgment will no longer be considered a lien against any real property owned by the judgment debtor. If your judgment becomes dormant and you do not revive the judgment within the time specified by law, then the judgment essentially becomes void and you would no longer be able to collect on the judgment by any means.

If a judgment owed to you is not paid, in order to keep the judgment active, see your attorney about pursuing an enforcement action before the judgment becomes dormant.

18.9 I restored my former name under my divorce decree. What do I need to do?

Generally, you present a certified copy of the final decree of divorce containing the order of name change to the agency where the record needs correcting, such as the Georgia Department of Driver Services.

The following checklist includes a list of people and places you may want to contact to inform them of your new name.

Name-Change Checklist

_____Banks and other financial institutions
_____Financial planner
_____Accountant
_____Creditors (mortgage company, auto loan companies, credit cards)
_____Credit reporting agencies

Name-Change Checklist (Continued)

_____Georgia Department of Driver Services
_____Department of records and vital statistics
_____Deeds and property titles
_____Stock certificates
_____Employers
_____Friends and family
_____Insurance agencies (homeowner's, car, health, life annuities)
_____Passport office
_____Post office
_____Public assistance office
_____Registrar of voters
_____Medical and dental records offices
_____Schools (yours and your children's)
_____School alumni organizations
_____Social Security Administration
_____Taxing authorities (city, state, federal)
_____Utility services (telephone, gas, electric, water, garbage)
_____Georgia Child Support Payment Center
_____Internal Revenue Service
_____Church/religious organizations
_____Frequently used service providers (stylist, lawn service, etc.)
_____Professional organizations

18.10 I was told by my bank that I need a certified copy of my decree. How do I obtain one?

Your decree remains permanently on file with the clerk of the court where your divorce was granted. The clerk will provide you with a certified copy for a nominal fee.

18.11 Is there anything else I should be doing after my divorce?

The following postdivorce checklist may be helpful in considering many actions that may need to be addressed:

Postdivorce Checklist

- Confirm necessary quitclaim deeds and real estate transfer statements have been filed with the registrar of deeds or clerk of Superior Court.

- Refinance real property within time frame specified by the final decree of divorce.
- Complete the exchange of personal property.
- Transfer the title on vehicles.
- Transfer or close bank accounts and safe deposit boxes.
- Transfer investment accounts, stocks, and bonds.
- Review beneficiary designations on retirement and financial accounts for any needed changes.

Property Settlement
- Comply with property settlement payments in a timely manner pursuant to your decree.

Insurance
- Review life insurance beneficiary designation for any needed changes.
- Obtain COBRA or other needed health insurance.
- Notify employer to maintain former spouse for six-month period on your health insurance, if applicable.
- Make sure your vehicle is insured in your name.

Debts and Liabilities
- Cancel joint accounts or charge cards, or remove name of former spouse.

Parenting Plan
- Notify child's school of the noncustodial parent's address and phone numbers.
- If you are the noncustodial parent, notify child's school of your desire to be notified of events, receive duplicate copies of report cards, and so on.

Child Support and Alimony
- If ordered to pay support, provide the original Notice to Withhold Income form to your employer.
- A new Notice form will be required each time you change employers.
- If ordered to pay both alimony and child support, include alimony information on the same Notice to Withhold Income form to be provided to your employer.

Child Care and Uninsured Medical Expenses
- Set up a tracking and filing system to keep complete records regarding these financial matters.

Tax Matters
- Notify your employer of the change in your exemption status (complete a new W-4).
- If necessary, complete IRS Form 8822 for change of address and also notify, if needed, the Georgia Department of Revenue.
- Refer to IRS Publication 504, Divorced or Separated Individuals, for other questions.

Attorney Fees
- Contact the firm's account manager to make payment arrangements for any fees owed to the firm.
- If your former spouse was ordered to pay a portion of your attorney fees, note that you remain responsible for the payment of your attorney fees, including any applicable interest, until the account is paid.
- If you have been ordered to pay fees to your former spouse's attorney, make payment using a method that provides you a means to prove payment was made, such as by check or a credit card. If you cannot make the payment on time, contact that attorney's office to try to arrange alternate payment plans.

Name Change
- Go to the Driver License department at the Department of Driver Services to get a reissued license with the change of name.
- Contact the Social Security Administration (SSA) (http://search.socialsecurity.gov/) to complete an Application for a Social Security Card (Form SS-5). Computer matching is done between Georgia Drivers Services and SSA, and if names do not match, a driver's license suspension may be issued. The SSA will notify the IRS of your name change when your new Social Security card is issued.
- Notify people and places regarding your name change. (*See* question 18.9.)

Estate Planning

- Review your will and any powers of attorney for any needed changes.
- Schedule an appointment with your attorney to update or prepare your will, powers of attorney, and other important estate-planning documents.

In Closing

Now pause and take a deep breath. Commend yourself for the courage you have shown in examining your unique situation, needs, and goals. Now, you are facing your future—recasting yourself into a new life. You are closely evaluating your living situation, the needs of your children, your financial security, and your personal growth and healing.

You are looking at your situation clearly and being truthful about your true needs. You are taking action to propel yourself into new possibilities. From here, it is time to take inventory of the lessons learned, goals met, and action yet to take.

Celebrate each of those steps forward and be gentle with yourself over the occasional misstep backward. You have transitioned through this time when everything is reduced to the core of you. Gone are the familiar habits of your marriage. With every day moving closer to the completion of your divorce, your grief will begin to subside and your energy improve as you move toward a fresh start.

Be mindful that many professionals suggest that just as a period of grieving is necessary after the death of a loved one, the death of a marriage likewise requires the same six months of healing to get your mind and self together. For at least that six months, avoid entering too hastily into any serious relationship.

All the best to you as you accomplish this life journey.

Appendix

Sample Complaint for Divorce

IN THE SUPERIOR COURT OF CHATHAM COUNTY
STATE OF GEORGIA

Jane Doe	)	
Plaintiff,	)	
	)	
vs.	)	Civil Action No.
	)	
John Doe	)	_____
Defendant.	)	

COMPLAINT FOR DIVORCE

COMES NOW Plaintiff JANE DOE by and through counsel, and files this Complaint for Divorce against Defendant JOHN DOE, and shows this Honorable Court the following:

1.

Plaintiff is currently residing at _____ Savannah, Chatham County, Georgia. Plaintiff has been domiciled in the State of Georgia for at least six (6) months prior to the filing of this Complaint. Plaintiff submits to the jurisdiction of this Court.

2.

Defendant is currently residing at _____ Savannah, Chatham County, Georgia, and has been domiciled in the State of Georgia for at least six (6) months prior to the filing of this Complaint. Therefore, venue is proper herein and jurisdiction over Defendant may be perfected, if necessary, by service of process upon Defendant as provided by law at _____.

Sample Complaint for Divorce (Continued)

3.

The Plaintiff and Defendant were lawfully married on _____ in Savannah, Georgia.

4.

The Plaintiff and Defendant separated on or about _____ and since said date have continuously lived in a *bona fide* state of legal separation.

5.

Plaintiff shows the grounds upon which this divorce is sought is that the marriage has been irretrievably broken, as set forth in O.C.G.A. §19-5-3(13), with no reasonable hope of reconciliation.

6.

There is one (1) minor child born as issue of the marriage, to wit: _____, born _____ in Savannah, Georgia. There are no other children born or expected to be born as issue of the marriage.

7.

Plaintiff shows that said minor child has resided with the parties herein since birth; that no proceeding other than this action has ever been initiated concerning the custody of said child; and Plaintiff knows of no individual other than the parties to this action who have any claim of custody or visitation rights concerning said child.

8.

Said minor child is currently in the custody and control of Plaintiff. Plaintiff shows that Plaintiff should be awarded joint legal custody of the minor child of the parties, with the Plaintiff having primary physical custody and the Defendant having reasonable rights of visitation.

9.

Plaintiff will hereinafter pray that Defendant provide temporary and permanent support for the said minor child, pursuant to a parent's legal obligation to provide the same according to O.C.G.A. § 19-6-15.

10.

There is no real property of issue in this marriage.

11.

The parties have acquired certain personal properties subject to equitable division.

12.

Plaintiff will hereinafter pray that the marital property be equitably divided and the marital debts be equitably divided, with due regard for who, when, and why the said debt was incurred.

13.

Plaintiff's monetary and nonmonetary contributions to the well-being of the family throughout the marriage of the parties has been substantial, but even after Plaintiff will have made as much progress toward self-support as can

Sample Complaint for Divorce (Continued)

reasonably be expected, the respective standards of living of the parties will be unconscionably disparate.

14.

Defendant has been the primary wage earner throughout the marriage.

15.

Plaintiff is entitled to receive temporary and permanent alimony from Defendant.

16.

Plaintiff is entitled to reasonable attorney's fees and expenses of litigation related to this action.

17.

Defendant is hereby on notice that Georgia law, O.C.G.A. §19-6-1(e), provides as follows in regards to transferring or disposing of property:

Pending final determination by the court of the right of either party to alimony, neither party shall make any substantial change in the assets of the party's estate except in the course of ordinary business affairs and except for *bona fide* transfers for value.

18.

Defendant is hereby on notice that Georgia law, O.C.G.A. §19-5-7, provides as follows in regard to transferring or disposing of property:

After a petition for divorce has been filed, no transfer of property by either party, except a *bona fide* transfer in payment of preexisting debts, shall pass title so as to avoid the vesting thereof according to the final verdict of the jury in the case.

WHEREFORE PLAINTIFF DEMANDS:

a.   A summons be directed to Defendant to require an Answer to this Complaint, if the Defendant desires to contest the dissolution of this marriage, again, said Answer, if any, to be filed with the Clerk of said Court and served upon Plaintiff's attorney within thirty (30) days from the date of such service upon Defendant;

b.   Service be perfected as provided by law;

c.   Plaintiff be granted a total divorce, that is to say, a divorce a *vinculo matrimonii* upon the legal principles between the parties;

d. The marital property and debts be equitably divided;

e.   That Plaintiff receive temporary and permanent alimony from Defendant;

f.   Plaintiff be awarded temporary and permanent sole legal custody of the minor child;

g.   That Plaintiff be awarded primary physical custody of the minor child and Defendant be granted reasonable visitation;

Sample Complaint for Divorce (Continued)

    h.   That Defendant provide temporary and permanent support for the said minor child, pursuant to a parent's legal obligation to provide the same according to O.C.G.A. § 19-6-15;

    i.   That Plaintiff be awarded temporary and permanent alimony from the Defendant;

    j.   That both parties be restrained and enjoined from transferring, selling, or otherwise disposing of any of the assets of the parties, except in the ordinary course of business and *bona fide* transfers for value; and

    k.   Such other and further relief as to the Court may deem just and equitable in the premises.

Dated this_____day of_____, _____.

                _____

                Richard A. Sanders Jr.
                GA Bar #
                Attorney for Plaintiff

327 West York Street
Savannah, GA 31401
RSandersJr@bellsouth.net
(912) 236-3020
(912) 236-1420 (Fax)

Sample Verification Page

IN THE SUPERIOR COURT OF CHATHAM COUNTY
STATE OF GEORGIA

Jane Doe	)	
Plaintiff,	)	
	)	
vs.	)	**Civil Action No.**
	)	
John Doe	)	_____
Defendant.	)	

VERIFICATION

PERSONALLY APPEARED, Plaintiff Jane Doe before the undersigned Notary Public, and who after being sworn on oath, says that the statements contained in the foregoing Complaint for Divorce are true and correct.

This _____ day of _____, _____.

_____
Jane Doe

Sworn to and subscribed before me by the affiant, whose Identity is personally known or proven to me by proof sufficient, This_____day of _____, _____.

_____
Notary Public
My commission expires:

Sample Letter to Spouse

Andrews & Sanders Law Office
327 W. York Street
Savannah, GA 31401

John Doe
1234 South Street
Savannah, GA 31401

RE: Jane Doe v. John Doe, Action for Divorce

Dear Mr. Doe:

This office has been retained by Jane Doe to represent her in the above referenced divorce matter. Enclosed is a copy of the Complaint for Divorce, which has been filed with the Court, and an Acknowledgment of Service.

By signing and returning the Acknowledgment of Service to my office at the above address you are avoiding the need to have a sheriff serve you with the above stated documents at your home or place of employment.

Kindly return the Acknowledgment of Service to my office in the enclosed envelope no later than fifteen days from the date of this letter. If I do not receive same by that date, I will assume you have no intention of signing it and will have a sheriff serve you as appropriate.

If you have retained an attorney, please ask your lawyer to contact my office. It is our desire to resolve this matter as amicably as possible for the benefit of you and Mrs. Doe.

Thanking you for your cooperation in this matter, I am,

Very truly yours,
Richard A. Sanders Jr.

Enclosures
cc: Jane Doe

Appendix

Sample Acknowledgment of Service

IN THE SUPERIOR COURT OF CHATHAM COUNTY
STATE OF GEORGIA

Jane Doe	)	
Plaintiff,	)	
	)	
vs.	)	**Civil Action No.**
	)	
John Doe	)	_____ _____
Defendant.	)	

ACKNOWLEDGMENT OF SERVICE OF PROCESS

The Defendant in the above styled action hereby enters his appearance and acknowledges personal service of the Complaint for Divorce; all additional service and process, including future service of summons, is hereby waived.

This _____ day of _____, 20__.

_____
John Doe
Pro Se

The use of a voluntary appearance is not appropriate for all cases, so discuss with your attorney the better choice for your case.

Sample Attorney Litigation Fee Hourly Billing Structure

Legal Services $250 per hour for lawyer time $125 per hour for paralegal time	Estimated Hours	Estimated Expense
Preparation of pleadings and orders including Motions, Stipulations, Decree, and Parenting Plan	5.0–10.0	1,250–2,500
Preparation for and attendance at pretrial docket call or pretrial conference	2.0	500
Discovery process: Prepare, review, and update: Request for production of documents Interrogatories Request for admissions Perform revised child-support guidelines	Paralegal–3.0 Atty–5.0	375 1,250
Ongoing communication with client and opposing counsel: Phone conferences Correspondence E-mail	Paralegal –2.5-6.0 Atty–10.0	312.50–750.00 2,500.00
Witness conferences: Initial interviews Screening Preparing for trial	1–4.0	250–1,000.00
Depositions (2-3): Preparation Attendance/taking Reviewing in preparation of trial	0–15.0	0–2,595.00
Legal research/memorandum of facts and law	1–5.0	250–1,250.00
Trial preparation: Witness preparation Direct examination Cross-examination File review and identification of resolved and disputed issues File review of supporting facts Evidentiary issues review Preparation and organization of exhibits including child-support guidelines, property, and debt exhibits Preparation of suggestions to the court Preparation of opening statement and closing argument	10.0–20.0	1,250.00–2,500.00

Sample Attorney Litigation Fee Hourly Billing Structure
(Continued)

Legal Services $250 per hour for lawyer time $125 per hour for paralegal time	Estimated Hours	Estimated Expense
Client preparation for trial: File review Agenda preparation Conference	3.0–5.0	750.00–1,250.00
Day of trial Final review of file Conference with client Court appearance at trial	5.0–10.0	1,250.00–2,500.00
Costs for: Court reporter, Witness fees, Subpoenas	Unknown	Unknown
TOTAL		**$9,937.50–18,970.00**

Sample Language from a Flat-Fee Agreement

a. The Initial Fee to be paid by Client is $2,500.00 for a divorce. The Initial Fee shall be earned by services performed which may include:

(1.) Accepting the case, initiating the file, reviewing the facts, advising on settlement strategy, conducting research as may be required to resolve preliminary legal issues, if any, and planning strategy to resolve your case.

(2.) Preparing, as circumstances may require, a Complaint and allied papers, attempting to negotiate an acceptable settlement, and preparing a Settlement Agreement, and representation at a Temporary Hearing, if appropriate.

(3.) Representation at a Final Uncontested Hearing, if necessary.

b. It is understood that said Initial Fee shall be fully earned by the representation provided, without regard to result, if any, that is achieved because attorney cannot guarantee final resolution during said period without the full cooperation/consent and good faith of both parties.

c. If the Court orders or the parties request Mediation, each daily session shall be attended for an additional fee of $1,000.00.

d. Client agrees, that if the case becomes contested (by either party filing a defensive pleading or answer) it may be necessary to take further action, if additional action is taken, Client shall pay Attorney additional fees as follows:

(1.) $1,000.00 for Attorney to prepare and send (each set) Interrogatories; Request to Produce; Notice to Produce; or prepare Answers to the other party's discovery request;

(2.) $750.00 for each deposition attended, regardless of the length of the deposition;

Sample Language from a Flat-Fee Agreement
(Continued)

(3.) $1,000.00 for each Court appearance before Final Hearing;

(4.) $1,000.00 for each Motion that is prepared or response filed;

(5.) $750.00 for any other Court filing, document requiring Court approval or extensive correspondence (other than ordinary);

(6.) $1,500.00 for preparing a Pre-Trial Order; Findings of Fact, or Proposed Final Judgment

(7.) $4,500.00 for a Contested Final Hearing before the Judge; and $7,500.00 for a Final hearing scheduled for jury trial.

e. Client agrees to pay any and all expenses incurred by Attorney or his representative on Client's behalf as the same accrue, including, but not limited to, filing fees, expert fees, court costs, official fees, court reporter/deposition costs, investigations, travel, copying of papers, postage, mileage, and long-distance telephone charges. The client shall pay a deposit of $300.00 for such fees upon request.

Appendix

Sample Family Violence *Ex Parte* Protective Order

IN THE SUPERIOR COURT OF CHATHAM COUNTY
STATE OF GEORGIA

Jane Doe	)	
Plaintiff,	)	
	)	
vs.	)	**Civil Action No.**
	)	
John Doe	)	_____ _____
Defendant.	)	

FAMILY VIOLENCE *EX PARTE* PROTECTIVE ORDER

The Petitioner having prayed pursuant to O.C.G.A. §§ 19-13-1 et seq., that a Protective Order be issued; and alleged that Respondent has committed acts of Family Violence and that Petitioner is in reasonable fear of the Petitioner's safety and the safety of Petitioner's child/ren; and it appearing to the Court that probable cause exists that family violence has occurred in the past and may occur in the future, IT IS HEREBY ORDERED AND ADJUDGED:

1. That these proceedings be filed in the office of the Clerk of this Court.

2. That this Order applies in every county throughout the state and it shall be the duty of every court and every law enforcement official to enforce and carry out the provisions of this Order pursuant to O.C.G.A. § 19-13-4(d). Law Enforcement officers may use their arrest powers pursuant to O.C.G.A. §§ 19-13-6 and 17-4-20 to enforce the terms of this Order.

3. That a copy of this Order be given to law enforcement and the Respondent be served with a copy of this Order and Petition for Temporary Protective Order instanter.

4. **That the Respondent appear before this Court, on the___ day of_____, 20____at_____ __. M. in room _____ of the_____ County Courthouse at _____ to show cause why the requests of the Petitioner should not be granted.**

5. That Respondent is hereby enjoined and restrained from doing, or attempting to do, or threatening to do, any act of injury, maltreating, molesting, following, harassing, harming or abusing the Petitioner and/or the minor child/ren in any manner. Respondent is not to interfere with Petitioner's travel, transportation, or communication. Respondent shall not follow, place under surveillance, or contact the Petitioner at any place of the Petitioner for the purpose of harassing and intimidating the Petitioner.

Sample Family Violence *Ex Parte* Protective Order
(Continued)

6. That the Respondent is enjoined and restrained from doing or threatening to do any act of injury, maltreating, molesting, harassing, harming, or abusing the Petitioner's family or household.

7. That this Court determined that it had jurisdiction over the parties and the subject matter under the laws of the State of Georgia and the Court ordered that the Respondent be given reasonable notice and opportunity to be heard sufficient to protect the Respondent's due process rights. This Order shall be presumed valid and pursuant to 18 U.S.C. § 2265(a) shall be accorded full faith and credit by any other state or local jurisdiction and shall be enforced as if an Order of the enforcing state or jurisdiction.

ONLY THE FOLLOWING THAT ARE INITIALED BY THE JUDGE SHALL APPLY.

8. That until further Order by this Court, Petitioner is awarded sole and exclusive use of the family residence at _____ _____.

9. Respondent is ordered to leave the family residence immediately and law enforcement_____ (sheriff or police department) is ordered to assist Petitioner in returning to the family residence and the removal of the Respondent. Respondent is to immediately surrender to law enforcement _____ (sheriff or police department) all and any keys, garage door openers, and other security devices to the family residence and law enforcement is to ensure that these are given to the Petitioner.

10. Respondent is ordered to provide suitable alternate housing for Petitioner and/or Petitioner's child/ren by _____.

11. Petitioner's address is ordered to be kept confidential.

12. Respondent is ordered to stay away from Petitioner's and Petitioner's minor child/ren's residence at _____ _____ and workplace at _____ or school and any subsequent residence or workplace or school of Petitioner and/or Petitioner's minor child/ren.

13. That until further Order of this Court, Respondent is restrained and enjoined from approaching within _____ yards of Petitioner and/or Petitioner's minor child/ren.

14. Respondent is ordered not to have any contact, direct, indirect, or through another person with Petitioner, by telephone, pager, fax, e-mail, or any other means of communication except as specified in this Order.

15. That Petitioner is awarded temporary custody of the minor child/ren, namely:

_____ DOB _____ sex _____
_____ DOB _____ sex _____

Sample Family Violence *Ex Parte* Protective Order
(Continued)

_____ DOB _____ sex _____
_____ DOB _____ sex _____

Respondent is ordered not to interfere with the physical custody of the child/ren.

_____Check here **only if Respondent** is awarded temporary custody of child/ren.

16. That Respondent is ordered to pay temporary child support for the minor child/ren to Petitioner in the amount of $_____ every _____beginning _____. All payments shall be made by or to: ____ income deduction order ____ child-support receiver ____ by mail directly to the Petitioner or _____.

17. That Respondent is ordered to pay temporary support for the Petitioner in the amount of $_____ every _____ beginning _____. All payments shall be made by or to: ____ income deduction order____ child support receiver ____ by mail directly to the Petitioner or _____.

18. That Respondent, **only when accompanied by local law enforcement,** shall be able to remove his/her clothing and personal items from the residence as follows:

_____
_____

On _____, 20_____ at _____ M.

19. That (Respondent)(Petitioner)(both Respondent and Petitioner) [strike through appropriate] is/are ordered not to sell, encumber, trade, damage, contract to sell, or otherwise dispose of or remove from the jurisdiction of this Court any of the property or pets of the Petitioner or joint property or pets of the parties except in the ordinary course of business.

20. That (Respondent)(Petitioner)(both Respondent and Petitioner) [strike through appropriate] is/are ordered not to disconnect or have disconnected the home utilities, change or have changed and/or cancel or have canceled auto, health or life insurance for Respondent, Petitioner, and/or Petitioner's child/ren or interfere with Respondent, Petitioner's, and/or Petitioner's child/ren's mail.

21. That Petitioner is awarded temporary sole possession of the vehicle: Make _____ Model _____ Year _____ Color_____. Respondent shall immediately surrender all keys, proof of insurance, and registration to this vehicle to law enforcement and law enforcement shall immediately turn over said items to Petitioner.

22. That Petitioner shall be allowed to remove the following property from the family residence for Petitioner and/or Petitioner's child/ren's use: _____

Sample Family Violence *Ex Parte* Protective Order
(Continued)

_____

_____.

On _____, 20_____ at _____ and law enforcement _____(sheriff or police department) is hereby ordered to assist the Petitioner during this removal.

23. That Respondent shall be required to return the following property for Petitioner and/or Petitioner's children's use: _____

_____

_____.

On _____, 20_____ at _____ and law enforcement _____ (sheriff or police department) is hereby ordered to assist the Petitioner with this return.

24. It is further Ordered

_____

_____

_____.

SO ORDERED this _____ day of _____, 20_____.

_____

JUDGE, SUPERIOR COURT

Sample Parenting Plan

IN THE SUPERIOR COURT OF CHATHAM COUNTY
STATE OF GEORGIA

Jane Doe	)	
Plaintiff,	)	
	)	
vs.	)	**Civil Action No.**
	)	
John Doe	)	_____
Defendant.	)	

PARENTING PLAN

(X) The parties have agreed to the terms of this plan and this information has been furnished by both parties to meet the requirements of OCGA Section 19-9-1. The parties agree on the terms of the plan and affirm the accuracy of the information provided, as shown by their signatures at the end of this order.

( ) This plan has been Ordered by the judge.

This plan   (X) is a new plan.
             ( ) modifies an existing Parenting Plan dated _____.
             ( ) modifies an existing Order.

Children's Name	Date of Birth
CHILD	OCTOBER 26, 2010

I. Custody and Decision Making

A. Legal Custody shall be (choose one):
           ( ) With the Mother
           ( ) With the Father
           (X) Joint

As joint legal custodians, the parties shall participate jointly in decision making with respect to all matters affecting the Child's growth, welfare, and development.

B. Primary Physical Custodian

For the Child: Child, born October 26, 2010, Mother shall be the primary physical custodian and Father shall be granted reasonable and liberal visitation.

C. Day-to-Day Decisions

Each parent shall make decisions regarding the day-to-day care of the Child while the Child is residing with that parent, including any emergency decisions affecting the health or safety of the Child.

D. Major Decisions

Major decisions regarding each Child shall be made as follows:

Educational decisions	( ) Mother	( ) Father	(X) Joint
Non-emergency health care	( ) Mother	( ) Father	(X) Joint
Religious upbringing	( ) Mother	( ) Father	(X) Joint
Extracurricular activities	( ) Mother	( ) Father	(X) Joint
Other_____	( ) Mother	( ) Father	(X) Joint

E. Disagreements

Where parents have elected joint decision making in Section I.D above, please explain how any disagreements in decision making will be resolved:

The parties shall at all times confer with each other on all the above referenced "major decisions," as well as on any and all other important matters pertaining to the welfare of the minor Child, with a view toward arriving at a harmonious policy calculated to promote the Child's best interest. If good faith discussions do not resolve the issue, then the tie-breaking authority shall be as follows: Mother as primary physical custodian shall have tie-breaking authority on all matters.

II. Parenting Time/Visitation Schedules

Father shall have reasonable and liberal visitation with the Child apart from Mother's residence at any time upon reasonable notice and mutual agreement of the parties. Father and Mother shall make every reasonable effort to accommodate the other with visitation at any time upon reasonable notice and agreement of the parties. During the term of this parenting plan the Father shall have at a minimum the following rights of parenting time/visitation:

(X) Every First; Third; Fourth; and Fifth weekend of the month.

For purposes of this parenting plan, a weekend will start at 6:00 P.M. on Friday and end at 7:00 P.M. on Sunday.

This parenting schedule begins:
(X) Date of the Court's Order

B. Major Holidays and Vacation Periods

At the time of the signing of this Parenting Plan, the minor child is not school age, therefore, until the minor child becomes school age, the following

Sample Parenting Plan (Continued)

Holidays and Vacation periods shall be based on the school calendar for where the child is zoned to attend school if the child were school age.

Thanksgiving

The parties shall alternate Thanksgiving holidays with the Child. On even years Mother shall be able to exercise visitation from 6:00 P.M. the day school is dismissed until 6:00 P.M. the day before school resumes.

On odd years Father shall be able to exercise visitation from 6:00 P.M. the day school is dismissed until 6:00 P.M. the day before school resumes.

Winter Vacation/Christmas/New Years

The parties shall alternate Winter vacation holidays with the Child. On Odd years the Mother shall exercise visitation with the Child for the first period, which is from the day and time school is dismissed until 2:00 P.M. on December 26th. On Odd years The Father will have the Child for the second period, which is from the day and time indicated above until 5:00 P.M. on the day before school resumes. The parties shall alternate the first and second periods each year.

Summer Vacation

Define summer vacation period: The Friday after school is dismissed for the summer until the Sunday before school resumes in the fall.

The Father shall have four-weeks visitation during the summer. He may have the weeks consecutively or non-consecutively. The Father shall provide written notice to the Mother of the days he intends to exercise visitation by May 1st of each year.

Spring Vacation (if applicable)

Define: The Friday after school is dismissed for Spring Vacation until the Sunday before school resumes. The parties will alternate Spring vacation— Mother gets Even years and Father gets Odd years.

Fall Vacation (if applicable)

Define: __ N/A __

C. Other Holiday Schedule (if applicable)

Indicate if Child will be with the parent in ODD or EVEN numbered years or indicate EVERY year:

	MOTHER	FATHER
Martin Luther King Day		
Presidents' Day		
Mother's Day	Every	
Memorial Day		
Father's Day		Every
July Fourth		

Sample Parenting Plan (Continued)

	MOTHER	FATHER
Labor Day		
Mother's Birthday		
Father's Birthday	Every	
Religious Holidays:		Every

Other: _____ The Father shall be entitled to exercise visitation with the child on any of the above-mentioned holidays, except the one specifically provided for, if he notifies the Mother of his intention to exercise visitation with at least two weeks' written notice (e-mail will constitute written notice).

CHILD'S BIRTHDAY: The parties agree that each shall have the right to have the Child celebrating her birthday with him or her for at least two hours on the Child's birthday each year. Said visitation shall be from 6:00 P.M. and end at 8:00 P.M.

D. Other Extended Periods of Time during School, etc. (refer to the school schedule)

N/A

E. Start and End Dates for Holiday Visitation

For the purposes of this parenting plan, the holiday will start and end as follows (choose one):

(X) Holidays that fall on Friday will include the following Saturday and Sunday

(X) Holidays that fall on Monday will include the preceding Saturday and Sunday

F. Coordination of Parenting Schedules

(X) Said holiday visitations shall have precedence over the regular visitation schedule but shall not otherwise modify it (for example, if the holiday granted in any particular year to a non-custodial parent falls between the regular weekend visitation the non-custodial parent will have visitation three (3) weekends in a row at that particular time.

G. Transportation Arrangements

For visitation, the place of meeting for the exchange of the Child shall be: Mother's residence or any mutually agreeable location

The Father will be responsible for transportation of the Child at the beginning of visitation.

The Father will be responsible for transportation of the Child at the conclusion of visitation.

Sample Parenting Plan (Continued)

H. Contacting the Child

When the Child is in the physical custody of one parent, the other parent will have the right to contact the Child as follows:

(X) Telephone: At reasonable times and for reasonable periods of time

(X) Other: The parties have a pattern and practice of e-mailing and texting each other.

TELEPHONE NUMBERS: Father and Mother shall each give the other a telephone number where the Child and the other parent can be located on a regular basis. In the event that either of the parents shall not be at his or her residence for more than a consecutive forty-eight (48) hour period, that parent shall provide the other parent with a temporary telephone number (which number may be the cellular telephone number of the other parent).

I. Supervision of Parenting Time (if applicable)

( ) Check here if Applicable N/A at the present time

J. Communication Provisions

Please check:

(X) Each parent shall promptly notify the other parent of a change of address, phone number or cell phone number. A parent changing residence must give at least thirty (30) days notice of the change and provide the full address of the new residence.

Rights of the Parents

Absent agreement to limitations or Court-ordered limitations, pursuant to O.C.G.A. § 19-9-1 (b) (1) (D), both parents are entitled to access to all of the Child's records and information, including, but not limited to, education, health, extracurricular activities, and religious communications. Designation as a non-custodial parent does not affect a parent's right to equal access to these records.

Limitations on access rights: __ None.

Other Information Sharing Provisions:

MEDICAL INFORMATION AND VISITATION DURING ILLNESS OF CHILD: Each parent shall be entitled to complete detailed information directly from any pediatrician, general physician, dentist, consultant or specialist attending the Child for any reason whatsoever and to be furnished with copies of any reports given by any of them to the other parent. Each parent shall be entitled to independently consult with all such health-care providers. Each party agrees that in the event of acute illness of the Child at any time, the other parent shall have the right of reasonable visitation with him or her at the place of confinement.

CHILD'S ACTIVITIES: Each party shall give the other reasonable Notice of any school holidays, vacation periods, special events at school, or other extracurricular activities of any nature such as parent open house, recitals, sports events, performances, or other similar events where parents normally observe or participate in the activities of the Child, so that each party may attend those activities.

CHILD'S SCHOOL RECORDS: Each parent shall be entitled to complete detailed information directly from any teacher or school giving instruction to the Child or which the Child may attend and to be furnished with copies of all reports given. Each party shall have the right to receive copies of all report cards of the Child, as well as copies of other documents and reports concerning the Child at school or to consult with the teachers and each parent shall so notify the Child's school. Each party shall have the right to notify the school of his or her desire for information and Notice, and the other party shall cooperate with such request. Further, each parent shall have the right to request that the school or counselor of the Child notify each of them of any and all teacher conferences or counseling sessions or meetings involving the Child and both parents shall have the right to be in attendance at such meetings so that they may agree, if possible, with regard to a course of action designed to nurture the educational and psychological development and growth of the Child.

IV. Modification of Plan or Disagreements

Parties may, by mutual agreement, vary the parenting time/visitation; however, such agreement shall not be a binding Court order. Custody shall only be modified by court order.

Should the parents disagree about this parenting plan or wish to modify it, they must make a good faith effort to resolve the issue between them.

V. Special Considerations

COOPERATION: This Parenting Plan cannot provide for every possible detail with respect to the custody of the Child. In that regard, the parties agree to cooperate and consult with each other so as to carry out visitation in a manner conducive to the best interest of the Child. Each party shall refrain from making derogatory or demeaning comments to or about the other in the presence of the Child. Further, neither will permit anyone else to make derogatory or demeaning comments to or about the other in the presence of the Child. Each party shall cooperate with the other so that the Child will respect each of their parents and neither party shall attempt to influence the Child not to love and respect the other parent. Each party shall keep the other party fully informed as to the health and whereabouts of the Child while having custody of or visitation with them as herein provided.

Sample Parenting Plan (Continued)

ENVIRONMENT: Each party agrees to maintain a wholesome and nurturing environment for the Child whenever having custody of or visitation with them as herein provided.

EXPANSION: Should the parties mutually agree to expand the visitation rights, then nothing contained herein shall limit or restrict the visitation rights as agreed. However, if the parties cannot agree, the Father shall have the right to visitation with the Child as described in this plan.

VI. Rules of Conduct

1. Neither party shall discuss with the minor child their past, present or future domestic relations litigation with the exception of the custody schedule and these rules of conduct.

2. Neither party shall complain about, criticize, blame the other in the present of the minor child, and shall instruct others to refrain from such conduct in the presence of the minor child.

3. Neither party shall accuse the other of being at fault in the presence of the minor child.

4. Neither party shall make negative, critical, and/or hurtful comments about the other party's family members in the presence of the minor child.

5. Neither party shall use the minor child to convey messages to the other parent.

6. The parents shall not hassle over visitation with the child. This undermines the parents' relationship with the child and burdens the child with the guilt of responsibility for such hassles.

7. It is beneficial that the child experiences affectionate care from both parents. The visitation privileges exist primarily for the child and not the parent.

8. The issue of visitation and child support are not related. The custodial parent shall not deny visitation to the non-custodial parent to enforce the payment of child support. Such denial is a violation of this Order.

It is the intention of this Order to relieve the minor child/ren of embroilment in his/her/their parents' controversies and disputes. Such conduct is injurious to the health and well-being of the minor child and will not be tolerated by the Court.

VII. Parent's Consent

We recognize that a close and continuing parent-child relationship and continuity in the child's life is in the child's best interest.

_____   _____
(Mother)   **(Father)**

Sample Parenting Plan (Continued)

We recognize that the parent with physical custody will make the day-to-day decisions and emergency decisions while the child is residing with such parent.

_____   _____
(Mother)   **(Father)**

We recognize that our child's needs will change and grow as the child matures; we have made a good faith effort to take these changing needs into account so that the need for future modifications to the parenting plan are minimized.

_____   _____
(Mother)   **(Father)**

We knowingly and voluntarily agree on the terms of this Parenting Plan. Each of us affirms that the information we have provided in this Plan is true and correct.

_____   _____
(Mother)   **(Father)**

ORDER

The Court has reviewed the foregoing Parenting Plan, and it is hereby made the order of this Court.

This Order entered on _____, 20___.

_____
Honorable Judge,
Chatham County Superior Court
Eastern Judicial Circuit, Georgia

Resources

Andrews and Sanders Law Offices
327 West York Street
Savannah, GA 31401
Phone: (912) 236-3020
Fax: (912) 236-1420
www.DougAndrews.com
E-mail: RSandersJr@bellsouth.net
Facebook: www.Facebook.com/AndrewsAndSandersAttorneys
At Andrews & Sanders Law Offices, our knowledgeable and attentive attorneys seek solutions to our clients' legal problems. We will focus on doing what it takes to provide zealous legal representation to pursue a positive resolution with loyalty to you and your cause.

Georgia Child Support Commission
www.GeorgiaCourts.org/csc/
For more information regarding accessing a copy of the law, informational materials, or tools used in calculating child support, please contact the Child Support Commission at childsupport@gaaoc. us. However, if you have specific questions about your own particular case, do not contact the Child Support Commission but instead consult with an attorney or your local Legal Aid or Legal Services office. The Child Support Commission office cannot provide you with any legal advice. Further, if you have a current case with the Office of Child Support Services, please contact their office directly. The Child Support Commission has no involvement with anyone's individual case.

Georgia Department of Public Health
2 Peachtree Street NW
Atlanta, GA 30303
Phone: (404) 657-2700
http://health.state.ga.us
Email: DPH-OpenRecords@dph.ga.gov
DPH is the lead department entrusted by the people of the State of Georgia with the ultimate responsibility for the health of communities and the entire population.

Georgia Legal Aid
www.GeorgiaLegalAid.org
For the section specifically on family law:
www.GeorgiaLegalAid.org/issues/family-law-and-domestic-violence/marriage-and-divorce
Georgia Legal Aid is a joint project of Atlanta Legal Aid Society, Inc. and the Georgia Legal Services Program. Georgia Legal Aid is a program designed to help low-income individuals solve their legal needs.

Georgia Legal Services Program (Savannah Regional Office)
6602 Abercorn Street, Suite 203
Savannah, GA 31405
Phone: (912) 651-2180
Phone: toll free: (888) 220-8399
www.glsp.org/regional-offices/savannah-regional-office/
Georgia Legal Services, an independent, nonprofit organization, provides free legal services to low-income people in civil matters in the 154 Georgia counties outside the five-county Atlanta metropolitan area. The mission of Georgia Legal Services is to work for equal access to justice under law for all people of Georgia.

State Bar of Georgia
104 Marietta Street NW, Suite 100
Atlanta, GA 30303
Phone: (404) 527-8700
Phone: (800) 334-6865 toll-free
Fax: (404) 527-8717
www.GaBar.org
www.GaBar.org/ForThePublic/
or

State Bar of Georgia (Continued)
Coastal Georgia Office
18 East Bay Street
Savannah, GA 31401-1225
Phone (912) 239-9910
Phone: (877) 239-9910 toll-free
Fax: (912) 239-9970
or
South Georgia Office
244 East Second Street / P.O. Box 1390
Tifton, GA 31793-1390
Phone: (229) 387-0446
Phone: (800) 330-0446 toll-free
Fax: (229) 382-7435
The State Bar provides a variety of information and services for the public—from consumer legal information to information about the attorney grievance process.

**State Bar of Georgia Local and
Voluntary Bar Association Directory**
104 Marietta Street, NW, Suite 100
Atlanta, GA 30303
Phone: (404) 527-8700
Phone toll free: (800) 334-6865
www.GaBar.org/AboutTheBar/LawRelatedOrganizations/LocalVoluntaryBars/index.cfm
Provides a listing of local and voluntary bar associations throughout Georgia.

The Superior Court of Fulton County, Georgia—Family Division
Administrative Office
136 Pryor Street SW, Suite C-826
Atlanta, GA 30303
Phone: (404) 612-0505
Fax: (404) 612-5582
www.FultonCourt.org/family/
Provide a comprehensive approach to helping families in crisis by using both judicial adjudication and service intervention methods. This site contains forms.

Glossary

Affidavit: A written statement of facts made under oath and signed before a notary public. Affidavits are used primarily when there will not be a hearing in open court with live testimony or at a temporary hearing where the number of live witnesses is limited. The attorney will prepare an affidavit to present relevant facts. Affidavits may be signed by the parties or in some cases by witnesses. The person signing the affidavit may be referred to as the *affiant.*

Alimony: Court-ordered spousal support payments from one party to another, often to enable the recipient spouse to become economically independent.

Allegation: A statement that one party claims is true.

Answer: A written response to the petition/complaint for divorce. It serves to admit or deny the allegations in the complaint and may also make claims against the opposing party. This is sometimes called a "responsive pleading." An answer must be filed within thirty days of either (a) the date the complaint was formally served upon the defendant or (b) the date when the defendant's voluntary Acknowledgment/Acceptance of Service is filed with the clerk of the court.

Appeal: The process by which a higher court reviews the decision of a lower court. The appeals process in Georgia family law cases is very complex and requires very precise steps to be followed. There are certain cases that can be directly appealed and there are other cases that have to be accepted or approved for appeal by the appellate courts (discretionary appeal). Georgia family law cases are either heard by the Georgia Supreme Court or the Georgia Court of Appeals.

Child support: Financial support for a child paid by the noncustodial parent to the custodial parent.

Complaint: The first document filed with the clerk of the court in an action for divorce, separation, or paternity action. The complaint sets forth the facts on which the requested relief is based.

Contempt of court: The willful and intentional failure of a party to comply with a court order, judgment, or decree. Contempt may be punishable by a fine or jail, or both.

Contested case: A case in which the parties litigate or contest the matters upon which they cannot agree, by presenting evidence, testimony, and witnesses to try to convince the judge or jury to rule in their favor. A contested case occurs when the parties have the court decide disputed issues.

Court order: A court-issued document setting forth the judge's orders. An order can be issued based upon the parties' agreement or the judge's decision. An order may require the parties to do or not do certain acts or set forth their rights and obligations. An order is put in writing, signed by the judge, and filed with the clerk of the court.

Cross-examination: The questioning of a witness by the opposing counsel during a hearing or at a deposition in response to questions asked by the opposing attorney.

Custody: The legal right and responsibility awarded by a court for the possession of, care of, and decision making for a minor child.

Defendant: The responding party to a divorce; the party who did not file the complaint initiating the divorce.

Deposition: A witness's testimony taken prior to court, under oath, and in the presence of attorneys and a court reporter. If a person gives a different testimony at the time of trial, that person can be impeached or contradicted using the testimony from the deposition. Statements made at a deposition can be used to show untruthfulness if a different answer is given at trial.

Direct examination: The initial questioning of a witness in court by the attorney who called that witness to the stand.

Glossary

Discovery: A process used by attorneys to discover information from the opposing party for the purpose of fully assessing a case for settlement or trial. Types of discovery include interrogatories, requests for production of documents, and requests for admissions. Usually, discovery is required to be responded to within thirty days of receipt of the discovery demand, except an extra fifteen days is allowed if the demand is served along with the original complaint. Discovery is allowed, in general, for all relevant matters in the case and for matters that may lead to relevant matters.

Divorce: The act of terminating or dissolving a marriage (in some states the term *dissolution* is used), and thereby allowing the divorced party to have the right to remarry.

Equitable division of property: The method by which real and personal property and debts are divided in a divorce in Georgia. Equitable division means that, given all the economic circumstances of the parties, marital property and debts are divided in a fair and reasonable manner.

Ex parte: Means "without the other party," or "one-sided." An *ex parte* communication between a judge and any lawyer or person concerning the merits of a case is strictly prohibited, except in very limited circumstances. An *ex parte* emergency hearing may be held if a crisis is impending and harm might be inflicted if action is not taken immediately. An *ex parte* proceeding, such as a motion hearing, means that only one party will appear before the judge, without the other party being notified or present. For example, an *ex parte* restraining order may be granted immediately after the filing of a complaint for divorce.

Final judgment and decree of divorce: The order that is signed by the judge and filed with the clerk of the court that finalizes your divorce and includes the obligations of both parties. This document signals the end of your divorce at the trial level and gives each party, technically, the right to remarry.

Guardian *ad litem* (GAL): A person, often a lawyer or mental health professional, appointed by the court to conduct an investigation regarding the children's best interest.

Hearing: Any proceeding before the court for the purpose of resolving disputed issues between the parties through presentation of testimony, affidavits, exhibits, or argument.

Hold-harmless clause: A term in a court order that requires one party to protect the other party from any loss or expense in connection with an obligation of the one party, as in "to hold the other party harmless from liability." Often, an indemnity (reimbursement) clause will also be used, so that if one party defaults in paying an obligation, the other party may make the payment (for example to protect a good credit rating) and that other party then would be entitled to reimbursement or indemnification for the expense.

Interrogatories: Written questions sent from one party to the other that are used to obtain facts or opinions related to the divorce action.

Joint custody: The shared right and responsibility of both parents awarded by the court for possession of, care of, and decision making for children.

Mediation: A process by which a neutral third party facilitates negotiations between the parties.

Modification action: A party's written request to the court to change a prior order regarding custody, child support, alimony, or any other order that a court has previously made.

Motion: A written application to the court for relief, such as temporary child support, custody, or restraining orders.

No-fault divorce: Grounds for divorce not requiring any evidence as to who is at fault for the breakup of the marriage. Divorce may be granted to one party or to both and no evidence of marital misconduct is required. This means that abandonment, cruelty, and adultery are not required to be proven for the purposes of granting the divorce. The divorce is granted solely on the basis that the marriage is "irretrievably broken" with no reasonable hope for reconciliation expressed by at least one of the parties.

Notice of hearing: A written statement sent to the opposing lawyer or spouse listing the date and place of a hearing and the nature of the matters that will be heard by the court. In Georgia, the party who schedules a court hearing is required to give the other party reasonable notice of that court hearing.

Party: Each named person in a legal action whose rights or interests may be affected. For example, in a divorce the parties include both spouses.

Pending: The period between initial filing of a case and up until the case is over, closed by a final order. For example, the judge may award you temporary support while your case is pending.

Petitioner: A term formerly used to refer to the plaintiff or person who filed a petition (now termed: *complaint*) seeking a divorce.

Plaintiff: The person who files the complaint initiating a divorce.

Pleadings: Documents filed with the court seeking a court order.

Qualified domestic relations order (QDRO): A type of court order that provides for direct payment from a retirement account (funds whose taxability as income has been deferred until a retirement eligibility date) to a former spouse, which must be done exactly as the retirement plan provides. A QDRO helps ensure the transfer of funds from one party to another party is consistent with the terms in the retirement plan itself and therefore not causing the transfer to be a taxable event or denied by the plan administer.

Request for production of documents: A written request for documents sent from one party to the other during the discovery process.

Sequester: To separate and exclude witnesses from the courtroom until they have concluded giving their testimony.

Setoff: A debt or financial obligation of one spouse that is deducted from the debt or financial obligation of the other spouse.

Settlement: The agreed resolution of disputed issues.

Show cause hearing: A chance to convince the court why it should or should not do what is proposed, including whether a party should be held in contempt for noncompliance with a court order or other requirements.

Stipulation: An agreement that something is true, as agreed by the parties or an agreement by their attorneys, with consent of the parties. A stipulation is binding and will not later be heard to be disputed.

Subpoena: A document delivered to a person or witness that requires appearance: in court, for a deposition, or to produce documents. Failure to comply could result in punishment by the court. A subpoena requesting documents is called a subpoena *duces tecum.*

Temporary restraining order (TRO): An order of the court prohibiting a party from certain behavior. For example, a temporary restraining (TRO) order may order a person not to transfer any funds or dispose of marital property during a pending divorce action, except for ordinary living expenses.

Trial: A formal court hearing in which the judge or jury will decide disputed issues raised by the parties' pleadings.

Under advisement: A term used to describe the status of a case, usually after a court hearing on a motion or a trial, when the judge has not yet made a decision but is going to contemplate it until some later time when an order or ruling will be issued.

Index

Index

Index

About the Authors

Douglas G. Andrews, Esq., is an attorney in private practice with the law firm of Andrews & Sanders in Savannah, Georgia, and admitted to practice in all the courts of Georgia, including the Supreme Court of Georgia, the federal courts, including the Court of Appeals for the Armed Forces, and the U.S. Supreme Court. He began his college studies at Armstrong State University in Savannah, Georgia, and completed a bachelor of science, *magna cum laude,* from Oklahoma College of Liberals Arts. Andrews then earned his Juris Doctor from Emory University's Lamar School of Law, Atlanta, Georgia.

After serving in the United States Army for twenty-two years, he retired as a lieutenant colonel. His military assignments included a tour of duty in the Vietnam War as an artillery battery commander assigned to the 199th Light Infantry Brigade, and he later served with the 82nd Airborne Division at Fort Bragg, where he earned jumpmaster status and senior parachutist wings. After serving in the Pentagon with the Office of the Judge Advocate General as a federal litigation attorney, and as staff judge advocate (senior legal counsel) for the commanding general of the Army CID Command, Andrews returned to Georgia for his terminal assignment as the general court-martial judge at Hunter Army Airfield & Ft. Stewart, Georgia. Prior to opening his private practice in 1991, he was the chief assistant for state court in the office of the district attorney for Chatham County, Georgia.

Andrews is an associate municipal court judge and is active in several veterans organizations, now serving as chairman of the Veterans Council of Chatham County, Inc. He is known for teaching lawyers, judges, and police officers in the classroom, and prosecutors in the courtroom.

Andrews has been married to Pam since 1969, when he met her while both were working at the Pirates House in Savannah. They raised three children and are now enjoying five grandchildren and one red-headed great granddaughter, who is the apple of everyone's eye.

Andrews may be reached through his website: **www.DougAndrews.com.**

Richard A. Sanders Jr., Esq., is an attorney in private practice with the law firm of Andrews & Sanders in Savannah, Georgia, and admitted to practice in all the courts of Georgia, including the Supreme Court of Georgia, the federal courts, and including the U.S Supreme Court. He graduated from Georgia Southern University in Statesboro, Georgia, with a bachelor of science in justice studies. Sanders then earned his Juris Doctor cum laude from Thomas Cooley Law School in Lansing, Michigan. He is a member of the family law section of the Georgia State Bar Association and the American Bar Association.

His primary practice area has been family law with an emphasis on divorces and custody disputes involving military service members and their families. He is also a registered mediator in Georgia for general civil cases and domestic cases. Sanders is judge pro tempore in the City Court of Bloomingdale and teaches in continuing legal education seminars for lawyers and judges. Andrews also coaches winning teams in high school mock trial competition, as well as mentoring moot court activities for the Savannah Law School.

Sanders is married to Crystal, a registered nurse, and they have twin daughters. They are also enjoying the twilight years of their "older child," Rox, whom some would call a dog (a boxer). Sanders may be reached through his website: **www.AndrewsAndSanders.com.**

Contact Information available at:
www.Facebook.com/AndrewsAndSandersAttorneys

Divorce Titles from Addicus Books

Visit our online catalog at www.AddicusBooks.com

Divorce in Alabama: The Legal Process, Your Rights, and What to Expect $21.95

Divorce in Arizona: The Legal Process, Your Rights, and What to Expect. $21.95

Divorce in California: The Legal Process, Your Rights, and What to Expect $21.95

Divorce in Connecticut: The Legal Process, Your Rights, and What to Expect $21.95

Divorce in Florida: The Legal Process, Your Rights, and What to Expect $21.95

Divorce in Georgia: Simple Answers to Your Legal Questions $21.95

Divorce in Hawaii: The Legal Process, Your Rights, and What to Expect $21.95

Divorce in Illinois: The Legal Process, Your Rights, and What to Expect $21.95

Divorce in Louisiana: The Legal Process, Your Rights, and What to Expect $21.95

Divorce in Maine: The Legal Process, Your Rights, and What to Expect $21.95

Divorce in Michigan: The Legal Process, Your Rights, and What to Expect. $21.95

Divorce in Mississippi: The Legal Process, Your Rights, and What to Expect. $21.95

Divorce in Missouri: The Legal Process, Your Rights, and What to Expect $21.95

Divorce in Nebraska: The Legal Process, Your Rights, and What to Expect—2nd Edition $21.95

Divorce in Nevada: The Legal Process, Your Rights, and What to Expect. $21.95

Divorce in New Jersey: The Legal Process, Your Rights, and What to Expect $21.95

Divorce in New York: The Legal Process, Your Rights, and What to Expect $21.95

Divorce in North Carolina: The Legal Process, Your Rights, and What to Expect $21.95

Divorce in Tennessee: The Legal Process, Your Rights, and What to Expect $21.95

Divorce in Virginia: The Legal Process, Your Rights, and What to Expect $21.95

Divorce in Washington: The Legal Process, Your Rights, and What to Expect $21.95

Divorce in West Virginia: The Legal Process, Your Rights, and What to Expect $21.95

Divorce in Wisconsin: The Legal Process, Your Rights, and What to Expect $21.95

To Order Books:
Visit us online at: www.AddicusBooks.com
Call toll free: (800) 888-4741

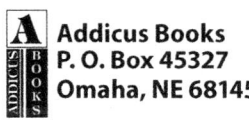

Addicus Books
P. O. Box 45327
Omaha, NE 68145